Learning from success

Improving practice and working together across health and social care

Parental Mental Health and Child Welfare Work

Volume 2

Pavilion

Parental Mental Health and Child Welfare Work, Volume 2

© Marie Diggins

The authors have asserted their rights in accordance with the Copyright, Designs and Patents Act (1988) to be identified as the authors of this work.

Published by:

Pavilion Publishing and Media Ltd

Rayford House, School Road, Hove, BN3 5HX

Tel: 01273 434 943

Fax: 01273 227 308

Email: info@pavpub.com

Published 2017

A catalogue record for this book is available from the British Library.

ISBN: 978-1-911028-70-3

Pavilion is the leading training and development provider and publisher in the health, social care and allied fields, providing a range of innovative training solutions underpinned by sound research and professional values. We aim to put our customers first, through excellent customer service and value.

Editor: Marie Diggins

Production editor: Mike Benge, Pavilion Publishing and Media Ltd

Cover design: Emma Dawe, Pavilion Publishing and Media Ltd

Layout design: Emma Dawe, Pavilion Publishing and Media Ltd

Printing: CMP Digital Print Solutions

Contents

About the contributors

Marie Diggins is a social worker. After qualifying in 1989, Marie worked for the London Borough of Lewisham and South London and Maudsley Mental Health NHS Trust until 2002. During this period Marie held a variety of positions including generic social worker, specialist mental health practitioner and, between 1995 and 2002, mental health integrated services manager. In 2002 Marie joined the Social Care Institute for Excellence (SCIE) where she worked with key stakeholders (government departments, health and social care staff, academics and service users and carers) to identify innovative approaches to embedding evidence about what works in health and social care in different practice settings. She made particular contributions to SCIE's mental health strategy and resources, including Think Child, Think Parent, Think Family: A guide to parental mental health and child welfare. She was involved with SCIE's digital production since its inception in 2007 and is experienced in the development of content for eLearning, film and other digital products. Marie contributed to Integration step by step, SCIE's digital resource to support integrated working, drawing on her understanding of practice development, practice contexts and multi-disciplinary working environments. While at SCIE, Marie initiated her PhD 'What works: Researching success in parental mental health and child welfare work', which she completed in September 2014. Marie left SCIE in 2014 and is now working independently as a part-time freelance consultant.

Kathryn Abel is professor of psychological medicine, director and founder of the Centre for Women's Mental Health at the University of Manchester. She is an honorary consultant psychiatrist in resistant schizophrenia and family therapy. Her interests include sex differences in mental illness; maternal condition and its effect on offspring cognitive development; parenting as a mediator of maternal effects and the outcomes of children of parents with mental illness. She has over 150 publications and has edited several books on women and mental health including *Comprehensive Women's Mental Health* (Cambridge University Press, 2016) and the upcoming *Female Mind* for the Royal College of Psychiatrists. She holds a prestigious European Research Council Science Fellowship, is a Senior Investigator at the National Institute of Health Research and the National Lead for Mental Health for the Clinical Research Network.

Jo Aldridge is professor of social policy in the department of social sciences at Loughborough University, and is director of the Young Carers Research Group. She conducted the first ever study in the UK on the experiences and needs of children who live with and care for parents with serious mental health problems and she has published widely in the field of young carers and parental mental health and child welfare. Jo is also a National Institute for Health and Care Excellence Fellow.

Jane Akister is a reader in social work at Anglia Ruskin University, co-editor of *Practice: Social Work in Action*, and an associate mental health act manager (Cambridgeshire and Peterborough Foundation Trust). Jane's research interests include family functioning, attachment relationships and parenting support.

Ruth Allen became chief executive of the British Association of Social Workers (BASW) in April 2016. Prior to that, she was director of social work at South West London & St Georges' Mental Health NHS Trust and also had a research role with St George's University of London. She has a particular interest and experience in leadership development in social work and in developing social work's role within mental health. Dr Allen holds a Master's degree in Social Work and a Professional Doctorate in Education, both awarded by the University of Sussex.

Kate Asaf has been a childcare professional for more than 15 years. For 12 years she worked as a learning and behaviour mentor within primary education, which involved supporting children and their families to overcome a range of educational, social and personal barriers to learning. Kate is also the director of Rocks and Pebbles Ltd, an organisation that provides wrap-around childcare in a number of primary schools throughout the London Borough of Lewisham. Through her roles and interactions with children, young adults and their families, Kate has supported a large number of individuals with mental health needs as well as supported individuals to understand mental health within their homes.

Claire Barcham is a social worker and approved mental health professional (AMHP) with more than 20 years' experience in front line practice. She has worked on both local and national levels promoting excellent social work across all ages, and she currently manages a generic out of hours social work team. Claire has maintained a special interest in the interface between adults and children's work, and provides training around the law in this regard. She is also the author of the successful The Pocketbook Guide to Mental Health Act Assessments.

Penny Bee is a reader in health services research and lead of the Mental Health Research Group in the Division of Nursing, Midwifery & Social Work at the University of Manchester. Penny's research interests focus on understanding concepts of health and healthcare provision from service users' and carers' perspectives. She has particular interests in user experiences, user and carer satisfaction and family support needs, and has conducted several studies evaluating new and innovative ways to overcome barriers to mental health care. Much of the research she has been involved in has been relevant to the academic field and government policy. She has been part of a team that has revolutionised the management of depression and anxiety in the UK, focusing on patient and professional use new psychological interventions (such as Guided Self-Help), which is the primary form of care for hundreds of thousands of people with depression, generalised anxiety disorder, post-traumatic stress disorder and obsessive-compulsive disorder. Penny has substantial experience in patient experience, qualitative research methods and externally funded, commissioned systematic reviews. She has expertise in the co-development and evaluation of child-centred psycho-educational mental health programmes and has been principal or co-investigator on a number of NIHR and MRC-funded studies developing and evaluating parental, child and family interventions for mental health. She uses creative methods to disseminate and engage the public in her work, and along with her colleagues, has won a number of awards for patient and public involvement in health services research.

Mandy Bell is a registered social worker who has worked in the development of young carers services since 1997. At Gloucestershire Young Carers, Mandy is responsible for the development of services, specialising in improving support to children caring for a family member with a mental illness and/or problematic substance. Mandy is experienced in delivering parental mental health/Crossing Bridges training. In 2010, a Winston Churchill Travel Fellowship enabled her to undertake a fact-finding trip to Australia, focusing on the children of parents with a mental illness. Gloucestershire Young Carers has used this learning to develop an award-winning whole family programme.

Lucy Brazener is the team manager of the Parental Mental Health Team, she is a mental health nurse and has worked within the PMHT since 2009. She has experience of working in both community and in-patient mental health settings and has a strong interest in arts and health. She is currently undertaking her MSc is Service improvement and Leadership and has been a part of the SLAM steering group in developing literature around mental health for staff, service users and their families.

Hugh Constant is a practice development manager at the Social Care Institute for Excellence (SCIE). He has worked in social care since 1993, and has practiced in residential, day care and outreach settings. He qualified as a social worker in 1997, working in the London Borough of Barnet with adults with learning disabilities before going on to manage a learning disability social work service in the London Borough of Tower Hamlets for six years. Here he led a major programme of change, focusing on improving practice and outcomes and leading a successful integration with NHS colleagues. From Tower Hamlets, Hugh joined SCIE. He led on several large projects, all focused on changing ways of working for the better in social care. He supported six local authorities across England and Northern Ireland to develop whole-family working with parents with mental health problems. He developed guidance and e-learning on assessment and eligibility, and on adult safeguarding. Hugh also worked extensively on advice and information services aimed at the general population.

Vicki Cowling OAM works as an independent practitioner in child and family mental health in Melbourne, and is an accredited mental health social worker and registered psychologist. Vicki has worked with children and families in government and non-government settings, including public child and adolescent mental health services in Victoria and New South Wales. She has also held positions in the field of mental health promotion, and since 1993 has conducted research concerning children of parents with mental illness and their families, leading to publication of books and articles, and most recently a thesis titled *Support for Children and Families Living with a Family Member with Mental Illness*, at The University of Newcastle, Australia. Over the years Vicki has consistently worked in partnership with family members including children, adult children, parents, partners and grandparents, and has also contributed to online professional development programmes for those working with the children and their families. Vicki was awarded the Medal of the Order of Australia (OAM) for service to the community, as an advocate for children of parents with mental illnesses, in 2005.

Sharon Crawford is head of service in Children's Services Northern Health and Social Care Trust (NI). She has worked in frontline safeguarding teams as an SW practitioner and manager since 1992. Her experience has been in the implementation of a gateway service referral model, work in child protection, looked after children and children with disability services. Sharon has been involved in the development and implementation of the NHSCT mental health and childcare champion project since 2008 and has a particular interest in the interface and practice between children's services and mental health services when families require support and statutory intervention.

Gavin Davidson is a senior lecturer in social work at the School of Social Sciences, Education and Social Work at Queen's University Belfast, Northern Ireland. Before moving to Queen's in 2008 he worked for 12 years in adult mental health services. His main research interests are in mental health including: the associations between trauma, adversity and mental health; social justice; the use of compulsory powers; and the interface between mental health and other services. He is part of the project team, led by Dr Anne Grant, that is working with the Health and Social Care Board to research the implementation of the Think Family approach in Northern Ireland. He is also the programme lead for Mental Health and Wellbeing within the Centre for Evidence and Social Innovation at Queen's.

Mary Donaghy qualified as a social worker in 1983. Over the past 30 years her experience has covered family and child care services (Residential & Fieldwork), children's disability services, and child and adolescent mental health services. Mary joined the health and social care board as a senior manager in 2009 to lead the regional 'Think Child, Think Parent, Think Family' project for three years. Northern Ireland was one of six national projects under the direction of the Social Care Institute for Excellence (SCIE). The project focused on improving collaborative working and enhancing a better understanding of multi-disciplinary roles and responsibilities of all stakeholders working across the adult mental health and children's services interface. Since 2012 Mary has been a social care commissioning lead for adult mental health and learning disability at the Health and Social Care Board, and she continues as regional lead for Think Family Northern Ireland. Think Family NI is now the core business of the Health & Social Care Board under the structure of Children and Young Peoples Strategic Partnership (CYPSP).

Adrian Falkov is a senior staff specialist in child, adolescent & family psychiatry in Sydney, Australia. He currently works at The Royal North Shore Hospital and private practice. After completing undergraduate studies in South Africa, he trained and worked in London (Guys, St Thomas' & Maudsley Hospitals) before moving to Sydney where he has worked in a number of clinical, managerial and policy positions. Dr Falkov is now a full-time clinician with long-standing interests in the impact of parental mental illness on children, family mental health service development, professional education, service evaluation (links between adult & children's mental health services) and the interface between policy and practice. These interests have informed family focused work in mental health services using The Family Model (www.thefamilymodel.com), which has been used in policy development, workforce capacity building and clinical work in England, Ireland, Europe and Australia to improve family focused practice in mental health services.

Lina Gega is a reader in mental health at the University of York, in a joint appointment with the Department of Health Sciences and Hull York Medical School (HYMS). She is a mental health nurse and a cognitive behaviour therapist (CBT), with a PhD in Health Services Research from the Institute of Psychiatry, King's College London. She has previously held leadership roles as: Course Director for CBT and Lead for Mental Health Nursing at King's College London; Deputy Lead for Psychiatry at Norwich Medical School; Research Ethics Lead for Social Work at Northumbria University; Clinical Lead and Commissioner for primary care psychological therapy services in Norfolk and Northumberland. Her track record is in digital mental health, while her current research focuses on interventions for children and young people affected by, or at risk of, mental health problems. She has led an industry collaboration that produced and evaluated an innovative virtual environments system for use in psychological therapy. She received a teaching excellence award and a teaching fellowship from King's College London.

Judith Gellatly is a research fellow/trial manager in the Division of Psychology and Mental Health, Faculty of Biology, Medicine and Health at the University of Manchester. She has worked predominantly in the mental health research field for 14 years. Her current role involves managing a feasibility trial led by The Manchester Centre for Women's Mental Health – '*Young SMILES*' – that aims to develop a community-based intervention to improve the health-related quality of life of children and adolescents of parents with serious mental illness. This piece of research involves working collaboratively with third sector organisations (NSPCC and Barnardo's) and the NHS. Her research interests focus on mental health well-being and quality of life, primary care mental health including brief psychological interventions, decision-making in mental health and psychological theories of health behaviour.

Anne Grant is currently a lecturer in mental health at the School of Nursing and Midwifery at Queens University, Belfast, and a registered mental health nurse. Her research and clinical interests include parental mental illness, early interventions for families when parents have mental illness, and workforce capacity in relation to family-focused practice. Between 2010 and 2014 she conducted a national study in Ireland that examined mental health nurses' practice with parents who have mental illness, their children and families. Since 2014 she has worked closely with the Health and Social Care Board (HSCB) in her contribution to the Northern Irish 'Think Family Initiative' and is currently Primary Investigator for a study commissioned by the HSCB to examine health and social care professionals' family focused practice across Northern Ireland. She is also a member of the Prato Collaborative – an international network of researchers (across nursing, psychiatry, psychology, social worker and sociology) who engage in research to inform service delivery and support for families when parents have mental illness and/or substance misuse.

Magne Haukland is currently working as associate professor in Bachelor's education in nursing and at the Master's programme in mental health care at the Department of Nursing and Preventive Work at Oslo University College and Akershus (Campus Kjeller). He is registered as a psychiatric nurse. Magne has been attached to, and participated in, the development and operation of several education programmes in the University

College. In recent years, Magne has been particularly concerned with empowerment, power, conflict, deviance and shame. He has published articles in several fields, but the main emphasis is on mental health work. He is a member of the Empowerment research group.

Anne Hexeberg, MSc strategic management, is currently working as adviser at Akershus University Hospital, department for research and development in mental health. Her expertise includes quality improvement, professional development and facilitating learning activities. She has several years of experience from higher educational institutions and specialist health services. Anne's interests are, among others, developing blended learning programmes, organisational learning, communities of practice and how to implement knowledge-based practice. She has collaborated with Dr. Adrian Falkov and Dr. Bente Weimand for several years on The family Model, and has played a vital part in the development of a Master's course on Families in Mental Health at Oslo and Akershus University College of Applied Sciences, of which The Family Model is the core element. She is now participating in developing an e-learning course of The Family Model as a conceptual model and practical tool, together with partners from Northern Ireland, Norway and Australia.

Diane Hunter is a social worker with over twenty years' experience of working within a range of children and families settings at operational and strategic levels. Diane is currently Development and Impact Manager in the NSPCC's Children's Services Directorate, taking a key role in developing and testing new services that aim to improve outcomes for children and afford a greater understanding about what works with a view to influencing wider change. As part of that role, Diane has led the development, implementation of *Family SMILES* a group work programme to support children who live with parental mental illness. She is now working closely with The Manchester Centre for Women's Mental Health who are leading the *Young SMILES* feasibility trial that aims to modify *Family SMILES* to create a community-based intervention to improve the health-related quality of life of children and adolescents of parents with serious mental illness.

Heather Kay is the schools' and community projects manager at the South London Gallery, where she has worked since 2011. She has developed the gallery's work with more vulnerable groups, particularly through the Supersmashers programme for looked after children, the Creative Families arts and mental health programme, and work with special educational needs and disability schools. She has spoken at national arts and health conferences, and has published in the *Engage* journal: arts and health issue. Previous employers include Pump House Gallery, ArtsAdmin, Wandsworth Arts Festival and October Gallery. She holds a Diplôme National Supérieur d'Expression Plastique (MA) from Grenoble School of Art, BA Hons Fine Art from the University of Leeds and an Art Therapy Foundation Diploma from Roehampton University.

Darryl Maybery from Monash University has over 70 journal publications and research grants totaling AUD3 million. His research focuses upon vulnerable families, particularly with regard to the impact of parental mental health problems on children. The central aim is to reduce the cycle of mental illness in families. In 2013, his research group were successful in obtaining a AUD1,855,891 grant to undertake the four year project 'Developing an Australian-first recovery model of parents in Victoria mental health and family services'. This program of research extends and rigorously trials the Finnish 'Lets Talk about Children' model in the family/community, adult mental health and rehabilitation sectors across Victoria. Darryl teaches in the area of research methodology and statistics and has a special teaching interest in program evaluation. Darryl was raised on a farm near Mount Arapiles in the Wimmera (Victoria, Australia) and lives in Gippsland with his partner (Andrea) and two teenage girls.

Chris McCree is a registered learning disability and mental health nurse with extensive experience of working in community mental health settings. Her current roles are an adult mental health liaison specialist in the London Borough of Merton and interim named nurse for safeguarding children in the South London and Maudsley NHS Foundation Trust, where she is responsible for the implementation and development of a Think Family approach that aims to enhance partnership working and improve the experience of families who access these services. Her previous role as described in the article enable her to bridge the gap between mental health and children social care services.

Daphne McKenna is an established multi-agency trainer with a proven commitment to effective collaborative working, having co-authored the SCIE parental mental health and child welfare guidance (Think Child, Think Parent, Think Family) and also their adult safeguarding e-learning materials. She has a proven track record as manager and child protection co-ordinator and uses these skills to raise practice standards in the delivery of training for the benefit of children and their families. She has worked extensively in the statutory sector and has more recently developed expertise in safeguarding training within the third sector.

Jane Melton PhD FCOT is the director of engagement and integration for 2gether NHS Foundation Trust based in Gloucestershire and Herefordshire, and Honorary Professor at Queen Margaret University, Edinburgh. Jane is a registered Allied Health Professional and was awarded a Fellowship of the Royal College of Occupational Therapists in 2012 for exceptional contribution. Her publications include a range of collaborative, occupation-focused, practice development studies, and she has addressed many international audiences during her career. Jane's interests include co-developed, integrated care, and she underpins her leadership with the principles of hope, inclusion and engagement.

Kate Moss is a specialist family worker at Gloucestershire Young Carers. Her background is in early intervention work with families and as a qualified teacher, working with children and young people of all ages and abilities. She has been helping to develop and deliver a whole family programme, in partnership with the 2gether NHS Foundation Trust, working with children and their parents who are impacted by mental illness.

Nhlanganiso Nyathi is a senior lecturer and course leader at Anglia Ruskin University, UK. His main research and scholarly interests are in child protection, interprofessional collaboration practice, professional judgment and decision-making regarding assessment and management of child protection risk. Nhlanganiso's doctoral thesis explored key influences to effective interprofessional collaborative child protection decision-making and practice. The research findings established the need for the systematic identification of child protection concerns and the systemic understanding of the collaborative child protection approach. Nhlanganiso has previously worked as Review Manager (child protection) and Independent Reviewing Officer (IRO) for children who are looked after. His post-qualifying work experience at practice, supervisory and managerial levels, in both statutory and non-statutory settings, includes social work for the London Borough of Sutton and Cambridgeshire County Council in the UK and as social worker for Bulawayo City Council and Government Social Welfare Officer in Zimbabwe. He was also the founding Chairperson for the multiagency Bulawayo taskforce on street children in Zimbabwe. Nhlanganiso also has human resource management experience with local and international corporations such as Anglo-American Corporation (UNICEM), Rainbow Tourism Group and British Vita PLC in Zimbabwe. Nhlanganiso is currently supervising undergraduate and postgraduate major projects and is a member of the Department Research Ethics Panel (DREP). He is also a member of the Faculty's Interprofessional Working Group.

Eleni Palazidou (MD, PhD, MRCP, FRCPSYCH) is a professor in psychiatry at St George's University of London Medical Programme, delivered by the University of Nicosia Medical School, Nicosia, Cyprus. She is also honorary professor in psychological medicine at Barts and The London School of Medicine, Queen Mary University, London, where she is involved in teaching and research. She worked as a consultant psychiatrist in the NHS for over 20 years and she is now an independent consultant psychiatrist based mainly at The Sloane Court Clinic in Chelsea, London. She is a member of the Royal College of Physicians and the Royal College of Psychiatrists (MRCPSYCH) and was awarded a fellowship (FRCPSYCH) in 2006. She has published extensively in peer-reviewed journals and she is on the editorial board of medical journals. Eleni has particular clinical and research expertise in the diagnosis, neurobiology and management of mood (affective) disorders (depression and bipolar disorder) and in psychopharmacology. She also has an interest in the interface between primary and secondary care and has been a psychiatric advisor to the World Association of Family Practitioners (WONCA) Working Group on mental health. She also has a particular interest in, and has been actively involved with, the Somali community, helping with the provision of mental health services both in the UK and Somalia.

Dendy Platt is an honorary senior research fellow at the University of Bristol. His contribution to research and development in children and families social work spans child protection, assessment of children and families, decision-making regarding children's futures, family support and parents' capacities to change. He has undertaken several empirical studies on the assessment of children and families, and has been involved in evaluations of the 'Newly Qualified Social Worker' and 'Early Professional Development' programmes. He has also been involved in a review of assessment-related research, and in testing approaches to the teaching of analysis in social work assessments. His most important recent work involved the development of a method for social workers to use in the assessment of parental capacity to change when the children may be at risk of harm (www.capacitytochange.org.uk). The approach was piloted through a collaborative knowledge exchange programme with three local authorities in South West England, and is currently the focus of commissioned practitioner training courses with growing interest from across the UK. Dendy's career has spanned both social work practice and university teaching. He has worked as a social worker and team leader in local authority social services departments, and in project director roles with Save the Children and Barnardo's. He moved into university teaching in the mid-1990s, and came to the University of Bristol in 2005.

Shula Ramon is the recovery research lead in the school of health and social work at the University of Hertfordshire. A social worker and clinical psychologist by training, she has been applying participatory action research in her work on mental health recovery, domestic violence, LGBT, shared decision making in mental health, and service user involvement in social work and mental health research. Learning from success is an integral key theme in her research, as well as in her PhD supervision work, and her teaching on the online MSc in Mental Health Recovery and Social Inclusion at the University of Hertfordshire. She has published 12 books and more than 100 articles in peer-reviewed journals.

Sarah Redsell is professor of public health, Faculty of Health, Social Care and Education, Anglia Ruskin University and Honorary Associate Professor in the School of Medicine at the University of Nottingham. She has an academic and clinical background in nursing and health visiting together with research skills in health psychology. Her research has primarily been focused around communication about aspects of health and well-being with parents of infants and children, which includes developing and testing interventions. Sarah has been the Principal Investigator for a number of externally funded projects exploring overweight and obesity identification and prevention during infancy.

Andrea Reupert is an associate professor at Monash University, Clayton, Australia, and director of psychology programs at the Krongold Centre. Her area of expertise is in vulnerable families and developing evidence-based interventions that support families through adversity. Her team is also actively involved in developing psychosocial resources for clinicians in collaboration with people in recovery. She is the editor in chief of the journal Advances in Mental Health, associate editor for Australian Psychologist, and has served as guest editor for the Medical Journal of Australia. Andrea is also the co-editor for an online resource, Gateway to Evidence that MatterS (GEMS), that aims to disseminate research in accessible ways to consumers, carers and clinicians. She recently co-edited a third edition of the seminal Parental Psychiatric Disorder: Distressed parents and their families. She has received funding from various philanthropic and governmental agencies for family-centred, inclusive approaches within an interdisciplinary and inter-agency approach.

Katie Riches qualified as a social worker in 2004 and since then has worked in various children and families teams across the South of England in both the statutory and voluntary sectors. Her most recent practice role was carrying out intensive community-based parenting assessments where she was often asked to give an opinion on whether the parent(s) would be able to make the changes necessary to safeguard their children. Katie joined the University of Bristol in 2014 as a research associate on a knowledge exchange project that aimed to develop a structured approach for social care practitioners to use when considering a parents' capacity to change harmful parenting behaviours. This project, led by Dr Dendy Platt, resulted in the C-Change approach. Katie remains involved in further developments of C-Change both as a researcher and as a trainer for Interface Enterprises.

Jennie Rose is post-doctoral research fellow in Public and Community Health, Faculty of Health, Social Care and Education, Anglia Ruskin University. Her research in the field of health psychology focuses on understanding and reducing health inequalities and improving the health and well-being of parents, their infants and children. She is currently leading a projects applying psychological theory to understand study recruitment behaviour, and the health effects for women of loneliness during pregnancy and early motherhood. She also works with Sarah Redsell on projects exploring overweight and obesity prevention during infancy. Her research interests draw on experience gained working with families in early intervention programmes in schools and as a mentor for families with children on the child protection register.

Paul David Spencer Ross is a senior information specialist within the Social Care Institute for Excellence (SCIE), which hosts the NICE Collaborating Centre for Social Care. Paul is a chartered member of the Chartered Institute of Library and Information Professionals and has worked on a variety of topics across the social care sector. He specialises in community facilitation and knowledge growth through information and resource forums for minority and unheard groups, along with practical training in searching skills for social care research evidence.

Rebecca Shute (MSc) is the head of profession for occupational therapy for 2gether NHS Foundation Trust based in Gloucestershire and Herefordshire. Rebecca holds a lead role in developing practice within mental health services which recognises and supports the needs of young carers and children in families with parental illness.

Nicky Stanley is professor of social work and co-director of the Connect Centre for International Research on Interpersonal Violence and Harm at the University of Central Lancashire. The Connect Centre undertakes research to prevent and reduce all forms of sexual, gender based and interpersonal violence against adults, children and young people. Nicky has led numerous international and national research studies. She researches on young people's and mothers' mental health, domestic abuse and child protection. She is currently working on a research programme examining the effectiveness of psychiatric Mother and Baby Units versus general psychiatric Inpatient wards and Crisis Resolution Team services (ESMI) and on a trial of an intervention for children whose parents have serious mental health problems. Her books address mothers' mental health, domestic violence and children and health and social care inquiries.

Dag Willy Tallaksen is currently working as associate professor at the Department of Nursing and Preventive Work at Oslo and Akershus University College (Campus Kjeller). He is attached to the Master's and further educational programmes in Mental Health Care and Health and Empowerment. He is registered as psychiatric nurse. Over the years, Dag has been a part of the development of new programmes/curriculums and teaching various education programmes at different levels related to mental health care, both in the University College and at other higher education institutions. He has been especially concerned with suicide prevention in the last 15-20 years and is involved in this work at both national and international levels. He has published articles in several fields, but the main emphasis has been on suicide prevention. Dag is also a member of the Empowerment research group.

Louise Wardale is a registered social worker with 27 years' experience and is Keeping the Family in Mind co-ordinator at Barnardo's. Her experience has included residential, field work, community development and strategic work across adults and children's, voluntary and statutory systems. Louise has worked as a senior practitioner in social work with Barnardo's Action with Young Carers Liverpool and for the past 13 years as the co-ordinator of an implementation plan for children and families affected by parental mental ill-health – 'Keeping the Family in Mind'. Grounded in the direct experiences of children and young people caring for and impacted by their parents' mental health problems, Louise works strategically to influence change across national and local systems, and across child and adult services. She was an active member of the Parental Mental Health and Child Welfare steering group, and a guest contributor to the SCIE guide, Think Child, Think Parent, Think Family. Louise is well known for the development of a range of resources, including the development of family rooms across in patient units and training materials produced in partnership with children, young people and families.

Wendy Weal is the managing director of Interface, a national provider of specialist expertise, support and training to transform the lives of vulnerable children and families. Wendy was the deputy delivery manager of the Families at Risk division of the Department for Education. She had a national role in supporting local authorities and their partners in setting up and running intensive family support services for families with multiple problems, parenting support and wider reforms around integrated services and 'Thinking Family'. Wendy was the national delivery lead for the Family Pathfinders and worked with other government departments and organisations to encourage and shape a Think Family approach. Examples include guidance on the development of local protocols between drug and alcohol treatment services, safeguarding boards and children and family services, offender management services, mental health services and young carers. Before this, Wendy was running a large housing department consisting of neighbourhood teams, anti-social behaviour teams and tenant participation. She was instrumental in setting up a successful Family Intervention Project, jointly working with partners, and in obtaining funding to increase and sustain the work. Wendy is a Level 7 executive coach and her passions include coaching, motivational interviewing and challenge and support. For more information about Interface visit our website http://www.interfaceenterprises.co.uk/

Martin Webber is a professor of social work at the University of York. He is a registered social worker with experience of working with adults with a learning disability and mental health problems. He is passionate about achieving social change through high quality social work and social care practice with vulnerable and marginalised people. His primary research interest is the development and evaluation of social interventions with people with mental health problems. This includes primary epidemiological or methodological work, ethnographic work to develop intervention models, and experimental work to evaluate the effectiveness of interventions. He collaborates with health economists, psychiatrists, psychologists and other health scientists to maximise the effectiveness of his research. He leads the International Centre for Mental Health Social Research and also has a growing number of PhD students who are working on empirical studies in social work. He has published over 50 peer-reviewed papers and book chapters, and is an author/editor of three books. His teaching interests are in mental health social work, research methodology and the practice implications of his research. He is currently leading a team of academics from the University of York and University of Central Lancashire, under a contract from Think Ahead, to develop and deliver a new social work programme for people with an interest in working in mental health services. At the heart of this programme is training to deliver evidence-informed social interventions, which brings his research and teaching interests together.

Bente Weimand (PhD) is currently a researcher and head of the research group 'Experiences of Service Users and Carers' at the R&D Department at the Mental Health Division, Akershus University Hospital in Norway. She is a registered mental health nurse with clinical experience from mental health services in adolescent acute settings, and adult long-term settings. She has acquired over 15 years' experience as a lecturer and head of mental health in nursing and mental health programs at different Norwegian University Colleges. She also has experience in developing blended learning programs and international online learning tools. Dr Weimand is currently a researcher and head of the research group Experiences of Service Users and Carers at the R & D department at the Mental Health Division, Akershus University Hospital. Her research interests include impact of mental illness and substance misuse on children as relatives, parental mental illness, family wellbeing, workforce capacity to engage in family focused practice and strategies to promote meaningful and effective engagement of service users, carers and the public in practice/services, research and education. She has taken part in several studies in these areas, and is currently involved in two large multicentre studies, on implementation of core elements of family focused practice, and on families' experiences on heavy substance abuse. She also co-led the Norwegian Health Directorate's development of national guidelines for health professionals working with service users' relatives within Norwegian healthcare services, which were launched January 2017. Dr Weimand is a member of various Scandinavian and international research networks that focus on children as relatives, parental mental health, and family mental health and thus broad international contacts. She is currently chair of the Prato International Research Collaboration for Change in Family Mental Health. Dr Weimand has collaborated with Dr Adrian Falkov for several years on the development of educational programs based on The Family Model.

Ragni Whitlock holds the role of clinical lead for family therapy and family-inclusive practice in Somerset Partnership Foundation NHS Trust. While her role is currently based within the adult mental health service, she has previous experience of delivering family therapy in child and adolescent inpatient and community mental health services for a number of South West NHS trusts and running a small private practice in family and couples therapy.

Editorial

Marie Diggins

This book forms the second volume of Pavilion's *Learning from Success* series, which acts as an update on key research, policy developments and practice innovations in the UK and elsewhere.

Research has established the potential adverse impact of adult mental illness on parenting, the parent-child relationship, the child and other family members, and the extent to which this poses a public health challenge. Problems with how adult and children's services understand and deliver support to parents with mental health problems, their children and whole families have also been identified. In contrast, far less is known about how parents with mental health difficulties and their children can be supported successfully.

This series represents a unique opportunity to address the gap in the evidence base as to 'what works' by drawing together a blend of researchers, policy makers, practitioners and services users to identify both opportunities and challenges as well as explore what works in which contexts, for whom and why. It is concerned with outcomes for parents, children and other family members as well as multi-agency staff and organisations.

Contributions cover adult and children's social work and social care, adult mental health and child and adolescent mental health, carers and young carers, education, training and workforce development from all sectors. The book looks beyond the UK and presents international evidence of incidence and experience.

To ensure we include material that is relevant and useful to the broad range of people involved, we have recruited an advisory board with considerable cross-cutting experiences of research and/or delivering or receiving services. I would like to take the opportunity here to thank each of them for generously giving their time and sharing their expertise during the development of this volume. A special thank you must go to Chris McCree and Lucy Brazener from the London Borough of Southwark who made it possible to include three chapters that depict different but connected elements of a wider multi-agency *Mental Health Think Family Strategy*. Details of all contributors can be found on p3.

These are challenging times for health and social care practitioners. The context for working in parental mental health and child welfare work remains critical. Child and adult mental illness continues to rise at the same time as many services are being cut due to austerity measures. With demand for services probably at its highest, and resources becoming harder and harder to secure or maintain, it is more important than ever that the resources that are available are used effectively and reach those most in need.

And yet, despite the difficult environmental context, or perhaps because of it, there are a growing number of examples of professional practice and service models that are breaking down barriers previously identified as getting in the way of sound inter-agency practice and whole family working, and generating new ideas about success. I am delighted that we have been able to include in this volume a range of research and practice examples that illustrate this.

To give a flavour of what you will find in this volume, Ruth Allen, British Association of Social Workers (BASW) chair and previous director of social work, provides the guest editorial, which gives a brief analysis of the role of social work and whole-family working in the context of individualised and segmented organisational systems and austerity policies and their impact on public services and on families.

The Family Model (TFM) (Falkov, 2013), which featured in volume one of this series, is being increasingly used in a variety of contexts and settings, and examples of TFM in action appear in each and every section of this volume. TFM supports family-focused practice by providing an overarching and comprehensive way of thinking about an individual's needs within their family. The first example in section one describes an international collaboration that is using TFM to develop and deliver a Master's level module for the Oslo and Akershus University College for Applied Sciences titled *"Mental Health Care" Program to improve Family Focused Practice*.

The first chapter in section two explores barriers to the inclusion of perspectives of parents with mental health problems and their children in research studies and the negative implications and missed opportunities arising from this. The second chapter examines the increasing number of grandparents that are now parenting their grandchildren and the impact this role change has on grandparents – including personal accounts of two grandmothers. The chapter concludes with an outline of implications for practice. The third chapter identifies what is known about the health related quality of life needs (HRQoL) and preferences of children and adolescents who have parents with a severe mental illness and looks at the associated development of a new intervention called *Young SMILES*, which aims to improve the HRQoL of children and adolescents. The final chapter in this section presents a systemic view of the relationships between families and professionals where there are child protection concerns, and explores how a systemic approach can be used to aid understanding of the family system and also to design appropriate interventions for the agencies and professionals involved.

Section three describes five different assessment, intervention and service models and their association with successful outcomes. The first of these is *Inter-Act: a whole-family approach to promoting the resilience of children of parents with a mental illness*, which embraces the principles embedded in TFM. In the second chapter, the pharmacological treatment of mental illness and the role of the family is discussed including treatment issues, physical health in the mentally ill, the role of the family and working together. The *C-Change: An approach to assessing parental capacity where children are in need or at risk of maltreatment* is discussed in the third chapter. C-Change is intended to offer a rigorous approach to assessing parental capacity to change, an aspect of assessment that has often been neglected in the past.

The fourth chapter looks at the Southwark parental mental health team, a nurse-led early intervention service that provides help and support for parents who have children under five and who are experiencing mental distress. The chapter includes interviews conducted with the manager of the team and a parent, giving examples of the range of outcomes for families that have occurred as a consequence of their involvement with this service. The final chapter in this section is about the *Creative Families Art Programme*, also situated in Southwark, which is an early intervention arts programme for parents experiencing mental health difficulties and their children. The evaluation methods and findings for this project are of particular interest and details of this and where to find additional information are included.

Section four examines the impact and effectiveness of two different specialist roles designed to improve family-focused practice across service divides. The first example is the Northern Ireland Champions Initiative, which aims to increase knowledge and skills for providing a family-focused approach and forms one component of a wider programme of work known as 'Think Family Northern Ireland' (TFNI). The second example is a personal and professional account about the creation of a mental health safeguarding children's manager role, and the contribution it has made to implementing and sustaining a Think Family approach in the London Borough of Southwark.

The research digest section in this volume has been compiled by Paul David Spencer Ross from the Social Care Institute for Excellence (SCIE). A useful tools and resources section is also included.

We believe that by starting with success and focusing on different perspectives about success, this book, like its predecessor, has uncovered some new ideas about what success looks like, how it is achieved, and what are the contributions and conditions most associated with successful outcomes.

Dr Marie Diggins
August 2017

References

Falkov A (2013) *The Family Model Handbook: An integrated approach to supporting mentally ill parents and their children.* Brighton: Pavilion Publishing.

Guest editorial

Ruth Allen

This excellent volume explores the interdisciplinary imperatives in working better to support and empower families – and each individual within them – when mental ill health or distress has an impact. It is a showcase of contemporary innovations and good practice, and it is heartening to see a revitalisation of this important subject in this volume, indeed in this whole series of journals. The articles here will challenge and inspire – challenge the still highly individualised approach to mental health support for adults and children, despite so much evidence telling us that recovery and well-being often lie in the combination of individual motivations and changes in the relationships of which they are a part. And inspire in many ways, but particularly in the diversity of applied and theoretical explorations presented.

The need to bring a family focus to mental health support is something that affects all aspects of the mental health system. The need to develop and maintain these capabilities across all disciplines in the workforce is incontrovertible. This is a shared responsibility across professions and across all parts of the mental health system.

In the last 15 years we have seen considerable advances in the recognition of good practice in how we work with carers, families and friends of those with mental health problems the UK, including parental mental ill health. We have seen improvements in legislation and policy regarding family members' and carers' (adult and child) rights and entitlements. This was given an important new level of recognition in English law by the Care Act (2014), which placed carers' entitlements to support on a par with that of people directly using services, and enabled the needs of carers, other family members and service users to be considered together, taking account of combined strengths and needs. The advocacy of carers and families themselves, and their representative organisations, has been very significant in this. Whatever we bring to this issue as professionals, its power is minimal compared to the persuasive self-advocacy and testimony of service users and family members about the importance of family and social focus, and the reality of the labour and love that family members and friends expend in relation each other.

As the articles in this volume illustrate, there have been considerable advances in professional understanding and models of practice, improving our knowledge of what we could be doing to support whole families with adult or parental mental health needs. But, from my own previous practice as a social worker and as a director of social work within the NHS, I know how hard it is to make good practice and policy intentions come to fruition in mainstream services. This, of course, is true of almost any national policy or practice shift. Implementation cycles are long and almost always underestimated by policy makers, commissioners and those leading implementation. This is certainly true of improvements in whole family working, which require a fundamental shift in mind-set, skills, definitions of 'success' and perspectives on human need, and which feels at times quite at odds with mainstream approaches.

As the director of social work in an English NHS mental health trust for many years, with a particular responsibility for our approach to carers, friends and families, I know how vital it is that inter-professional collaboration includes a shared commitment to positive approaches to the social and kinship networks around the 'client', or 'patient', whether child or adult. This needs to be embedded in the culture, practices and emotional norms of the organisation.

From specific family-focused interventions and models of support to the information we need in order to provide ways that are accessible to family members of all ages, through the way we simply make time to call back when a family member leaves a message, to how we integrate the needs and capabilities of children and young people into the work we do with their parents or care givers, to the way we ensure we listen closely and offer authentic, honest collaboration with families, a carer, friend and family approach needs to be at the heart of all inter-disciplinary services and networks of mental health support.

Our unsuitable organisational systems and cultures

If a family-focused, family inclusive, relationship-aware approach to mental health support is our destination, too few of our organisational vehicles and maps for getting there are fit for purpose. Our assessment, diagnostic and treatment processes still tend to the medically reductive, locating the dysfunction and the locus of intervention overwhelmingly in the individual. In the UK health system, recording, information systems and local and national performance measures still drive individualised approaches and the segmentation of our understanding of needs into distinct categories of 'adult', 'child', or 'older people' within health and social care.

Professionals develop and work in specialisms (often for very good, evidence-based reasons) and can provide vital, focused support to individuals in many important ways. Dyadic therapies, individual advocacy, carefully boundaried confidential disclosure settings, one-to-one clinical consultations; these all have their place. But services are too dominated by decontextualised models of individual intervention, categorised by age, 'condition' or 'care group', as if people do not live, thrive and suffer in ways that are fundamentally shaped through their relationships with others and the social roles they fulfil, often with complex intersecting needs and identities. These dominant models of care within our mainstream public institutions are too often structured to miss the relationship-based human realities that can either be the strongest factors in recovery – or contributors to ongoing distress – with which practitioners need to interact.

Social work and whole-family working

It is something of a truism within contemporary social work that we claim to be the profession (above others) that is particularly focused on relationships, families, social networks and communities rather than just individual needs. This is, of course, in part because of social work's specialist role in child protection and 'family work', but it goes beyond that to the claim of a family focus and (often) a 'systemic lens' whether the identified client is an adult or child.

Whether the evidence in social work with adults and children across the UK yet lives up to our claim of a distinct family and systemic approach may be debateable. We are, for instance, only recently emerging from years of individual, consumerist 'care management' in adults services and our role here has been too frequently constrained by delivering individualised activities under the care programme approach, often missing the significance of whole-family relationships and the needs of all within that social system. But our claim to having well-developed, whole-family (and wider social network) approaches significantly – and to my mind, rightly – shapes our ambitions and intentions for the future of the profession, and there are plenty of excellent examples of relationship-focused practice emerging across the child and adult social work landscape.

UK social work's claim to a particularly skilled focus on family and social relationships has its roots in the fact that social workers have over recent decades undertaken generic qualifying educational programmes that cover the whole life course and, after the Seebohm reforms of the 1970s through to the 1990s, social workers often took generic statutory job roles within local authorities, frequently serving families as a whole as well as individuals of different ages and with different needs. Often working in 'patch-based' services, a social worker could develop a strong understanding of the local context of people's lives, their neighbourhoods and their communities.

The particular value of social work is often described in terms of our grounding in these practice skills across the lifespan with adults, children and families, coupled with our sociological and socio-political understanding of how people's circumstances and welfare are affected by wider structural and systemic (societal) factors such as wealth, employment, education, discrimination, inequalities, culture, religion and civic inclusion. As Professor David Croisdale-Appleby's review of social work education stated in 2014, social workers may be described as 'practitioners, professionals and social scientists'[1].

Recent governmental policy in the education and statutory employment of social workers in England has widened the adults/children and families divide in social work. Many educationalists, professional leaders and representative bodies see a pressing need to resist this division and reassert the importance of social work as 'one profession' with common sociological, community and family and group relations perspectives at its heart, albeit with many specialisms and job roles.

A pressing contemporary need to restate and, indeed, to defend the importance of this 'one profession' and sociological perspective on social work – particularly in England – has been created by the Conservative (and previous Coalition) government's moves to promote specialised qualifying training with a strong emphasis on child protection social work training potentially to the detriment of other areas of practice.

1 Croisdale-Appleby D (2014) *Re-visioning Social Work Education: An independent review.* London: Department of Health.

Current governmental policy towards social work in England also appears to be focused on de-emphasising the profession's role in revealing and addressing the social and economic determinants of well-being and distress. Michael Gove, when Secretary of State for Education in 2013, said that, 'in too many cases, social work training involves idealistic students being told that the individuals with whom they will work have been disempowered by society. They will be encouraged to see these individuals as victims of social injustice whose fate is overwhelmingly decreed by the economic forces and inherent inequalities which scar our society. This analysis is, sadly, as widespread as it is pernicious.'

This type of discourse caricatures social workers as making excuses and overlooking risks towards children. The evidence of the comparative safety of the English (and wider UK) child protection system does not bear this out. Nor does the appetite for, and engagement with innovations in good practice and skills development, and the combination of compassion and realism that characterises mature and effective social work. However, social work does indeed have a critique of the socio-economic and political contexts in which family and individual needs arise. And this has never been more pertinent and important for the profession to voice.

Austerity

Cutting across professional opportunities to learn from and implement innovations in more effective whole-family practice – across much of the Western world – is the impact of austerity policies and continuing weaknesses in many parts of the economy that are biting into both levels of service provision and worsening socio-economic life chances for millions of families.

The impact of welfare reforms on adults and children in the UK cannot be underestimated. This includes reforms such as the total benefits 'cap', the 'bedroom tax' (which judges whether additional bedrooms in a property are 'necessary' and imposes reductions in housing benefit if they are deemed not to be), stringent work capability assessments for disabled people, reductions in 'in-work' tax credits and benefits, and job seeker benefits 'sanctions', which can be applied when people make even small administrative 'errors', for example in evidencing their efforts to find work.

This ideological shift in public policy has gone alongside cuts in funding for public health and social care services. Adult social care funding has been cut across England by over a third since 2010 relative to demand. While overall cuts in statutory children's social care have not been as great, investment has dropped in real terms as demand has grown in most localities, numbers of children being accommodated has increased, and social work caseloads have remained too high in most authorities.

Even where statutory child protection services have retained or even increased funding levels, overall severe budgetary pressures in local authorities have significantly reduced early help services for families. Increasing evidence points to the particular detriment being experienced by parents with mental health needs, learning disabilities, those experiencing domestic violence, those who are in poverty, and those who are at particular risk of child protection actions being taken including having children permanently accommodated or adopted.

For instance, the Council of Europe was particularly critical of the UK in 2015 for the removal of children from women subject to domestic violence or depression. In 2016, the Joseph Rowntree Foundation published a major evidence review of the relationship between poverty, child abuse and neglect in the UK[2]. This identified a significant reduction in early-help strategies for families, and highlighted the immediate and lifelong emotional and financial cost of not providing such early help. It concluded that: there is a lack of joined-up thinking and action about poverty, child abuse and neglect in the UK at policy level; that the UK evidence base is limited both in terms of official data and research; and lessening family poverty across the population is likely to have a positive effect on reducing child abuse and neglect and its wider social and financial impacts on society.

Some implications for whole-family working

This brief analysis of the impact of austerity policies on public services and on families implies that change towards family-focused practice is being hampered not only by organisational, professional and cultural barriers, but also by severe funding reductions, widening inequalities and the rolling back of public care and health services in the UK, as across many Western democracies. This is undermining the availability of specialist social care and mental health services, statutory and non-statutory, and also universal preventive and primary care services. It is also undermining professionals' abilities to use their discretion and to take the time that is often needed to gain skills and practice with whole families in mind, which keeps caseloads high and focuses efforts on statutory risks rather than family development potential.

We are working with more families under increased social and economic stress, with fewer resources. We cannot divorce our enthusiasm for better practice models and priorities from the worsening socio-economic context in which family needs arise and within which multidisciplinary professionals must work. As practitioners of all disciplines develop their skills with families, as illustrated in the examples in this volume, it is important we also keep our gaze up and maintain our perspective on whether and how wider social and economic policies are contributing to the difficulties people face. And, as multidisciplinary professionals, we need to work together – with experts by experience – to ensure our evidence of good practice, and the challenges to working in accordance with that evidence caused by austerity, are heard by policy makers and politicians.

---

2 Bywaters P, Bunting L, Davidson G, Hanratty J, Mason W, McCartan C & Steils N (2016) *The Relationship Between Poverty, Child Abuse and Neglect: An evidence review* [online]. York: Joseph Rowntree Foundation. Available at: https://www.jrf.org.uk/report/relationship-between-poverty-child-abuse-and-neglect-evidence-review (accessed June 2017).

Education and training

Integration of the Family Model into educational programs

Development of 'The Family in Mental Health' module for the Oslo and Akershus University College Masters in mental health programme.

Bente M Weimand, Anne Hexeberg, Dag Willy Tallaksen, Magne Haukland, Anne Grant and Adrian Falkov

Introduction: an international collaborative effort to improve family-focused practice

This chapter describes an international collaboration to develop and deliver a Master's level module (10 ECTS) using the Family Model (TFM) for the Oslo and Akershus University College for Applied Sciences Masters 'Mental Health Care' Programme. The development, content, implementation and brief evaluation of the module for the 'Families in mental health care' course will be presented, together with the ways in which TFM was used as the conceptual framework (Falkov, 2012; Falkov, 2015).

The course targets new and existing employees working in municipalities, specialist health services (public and private sectors) and non-governmental organisations (NGOs), as well as inpatient, outpatient and community mental health settings. Eligibility includes those with a bachelor's degree in health and welfare studies, with a nursing, social work, midwifery, allied health and pedagogy background. The course is also relevant to psychologists, physicians and psychiatrists.

In addition to the chapter authors, a Norwegian reference group was established with representatives from:

➔ NGOs: Voksne for barn (Adults for Children): Gro Kristiansen and Merethe Toft, and LPP (National Association of Families in Mental Health): Kenneth Lien Steen and Anne Sund;

➔ National Competence Center: Nasjonalt senter for Erfaringskompetanse innen psykisk helse (National Center for Experiential Expertise in Mental Health): Eva Svendsen;

➔ Clinicians from mental health services at Akershus University Hospital: Linn E. Hanssen and Madeleine B. Corneliussen; and Health services in Municipality Ullensaker: Karin Gedde.

The primary aim is to provide a comprehensive, experiential course to improve awareness, knowledge and skills about why and how to involve and support families in mental health services, and to ensure active skills transfer from theory to practice, based on TFM and its six domains.

The first course was delivered in 2016 and details, including feedback from participants, will be provided.

Background

Although families and relatives are an integral part of society's overall care resource, their contribution is frequently hidden. The burden of care also puts the relatives' own health (both physical and mental) at risk (Weimand *et al*, 2010; Weimand, 2012; Ewertzon *et al*, 2012; Johansson *et al*, 2015; Kletthagen, 2015) and many live with significant emotional strain, as well as practical, social and economic challenges, which, together, can limit participation in education, employment and social connectedness.

Family interventions have been shown to benefit the affected individual's illness course (Bird, 2010) as well as improving the whole family's understanding (Okpokoro *et al*, 2014). Children and minor siblings as relatives also constitute an especially vulnerable group and warrant specific focus, given their own developmental and associated mental health needs (Beardsley *et al*, 1998; Smith, 2004). Stress from parenting may have a negative impact on parental mental health (Grant, 2014). Parental difficulties in meeting children's needs and ensuring their safety are further challenges (Siegenthaler *et al*, 2012; Smith, 2004), but not all individuals or families will inevitably experience difficulties, given the dynamic interplay between resilience and vulnerability. The mental health of adults with childcare responsibilities is therefore acknowledged as a global public health issue (Siegenthaler *et al*, 2012; Falkov *et al*, 2016) requiring greater focus on individuals within their family context and systematic implementation of family-focused practice (ibid.; Maybery & Reupert, 2009).

However, challenges and barriers in definition and delivery of family-focused care in mental health services are well described (Foster *et al*, 2016) and workforce education and training is a key component in the paradigm shift required to achieve a systematic family focus in mental health services (Weimand, 2012; Weimand *et al*, 2013).

In Norway there has been increasing recognition of the need for family-focused practice in mental health services for a number of years. This focus has been facilitated by Norwegian legislation and health policies, which recognise the roles and challenges for adult caregivers and the need to identify, register and support children as relatives. This includes promoting mental health and preventing mental illness in this group of at risk families. More recent guidelines ensure a legal mandate for staff in the health and care services to ensure appropriate involvement and support for these families (Norwegian Directorate of Health, 2010). However, to date, the presence of both policy and legislation alone has been insufficient to address systematically the needs of all family members when an adult parent is experiencing mental illness, and multiple barriers remain.

Need for a course that facilitates professionals to implement family-focused practice in mental health services in Norway

The development of the course was informed by the need for a program that:

→ focuses explicitly on family needs, including responsibilities for sharing information and how to provide appropriate, developmentally informed support

→ was more accessible and cost effective than existing family therapy programmes

→ conveyed a systems approach to working with families that is readily understandable, practical and able to be used in a variety of settings, by staff with different skill and experience levels

→ addresses the gap in the educational provision in this area

→ emphasises practical utility – achievement of clinical competencies about how to meet, communicate with and support families within mental health services.

The Norwegian authors decided to develop a Master's course that would contribute substantially to the above-mentioned requirements for health service personnel and managers. They believed TFM could provide the basis for such a course. In their view, TFM was well suited for the educational purposes outlined earlier. The simplified, visual structure allows for an understanding of basic approaches, supports a way of structuring knowledge and targets what health personnel need to know and understand about relationships and social connections. It can also be used as a practical (clinical) tool to support family-focused practice and the development of collaborative/family care plans.

The Family Model

'The links between mental health and parenting thus begin early in life, are evident across the lifespan, and are an important determinant of health and social outcomes in succeeding generations.' (Falkov, 2012)

TFM supports family-focused practice by providing an overarching and comprehensive way of thinking about an individual's needs within their family and social context.

Its theoretical underpinnings are drawn from the biopsychosocial and developmental approaches used to better represent the complexities of multiple systems in which human beings develop and in which mental illness occurs. The approach thus represents a more integrated understanding, incorporating mental health, human development, family relationships and parenting, together with a service interface and ecological wrap-around.

The concept of 'family' is understood in a broad sense and not only as the nuclear family, with relationships – interactions between key individuals – being the core focus.

By linking the various domains relevant to mentally ill individuals within their family and social context, the intention is to create an approach suitable for staff of varying experience and professional backgrounds, working in diverse settings across different agencies. This approach incorporates the proximal influences and interactions of an individual within the family, as well as more distal relationships such as neighbourhood and religious networks, as well as schools, cultural and societal values and aspirations. TFM is therefore eclectic and 'non-denominational' in drawing from existing models and providing a broader, more integrated approach (Reupert *et al*, 2015).

A visual approach

TFM is a visual illustration of the key areas or elements (called 'Domains') involved in understanding how mental/physical illness in one family member can affect others and how they, through their understanding and responses, can in turn influence the experience of the unwell person. It emphasises the reciprocal role of relationships in determining both good and poor outcomes for all family members. For example:

→ Being a parent/carer experiencing mental/physical ill-health can affect parenting, the inter-parental relationship and interactions with children.

→ Children and young people's mental and physical ill-health and/or developmental needs can impact on parents and other family members in various ways.

TFM demonstrates the key areas of focus and associated interactions using six Domains and 10 bidirectional arrows (Figure 1). A developmental perspective is illustrated with multiple cross sectional 'slices' of the TFM (see Figure 4).

The six Domains are as follows:

Domain 1: Adult/parental mental illness

Domain 2: Child mental health and development

Domain 3: Family relationships (parenting & marital interactions)

Domain 4: Risk & protective factors

Domain 5: Services for children & adults

Domain 6: Cultural & community influences

Figure 4 shows the cross-sectional 'slices' of TFM and looks at the life-span of an individual:

1. Looking at the present:
   → Living with mental illness

2. Looking back:
   → Childhood origins of adult psychopathology.

3. Looking ahead (incorporating present and past issues into treatment and care planning processes):
   → Assessment (collect contemporary and historical/ background information).
   → Risk management.
   → Treatment and prevention of relapse.
   → Planning (family focused) services.

In the opinion of the authors, TFM could be used at four levels within health services, as a tool to guide the clinical process. The course content addresses all levels and helps students to acquire a better appreciation of the organisational structures, barriers and ways of implementing family-focused practice.

Level 1:

→ In assessment of patients and family needs and monitoring health service responses (individual and family care plan).

→ By supporting conversations with patients about links between their illness and the impact on children.

→ By informing/guiding patient-parents about how to talk with children about their illness.

Level 2:

→ In therapeutic family conversations.

→ By assisting child-responsible personnel in monitoring staff and families progress.

Level 3:

→ In planning follow-up of patients and families, in partnership with local community and specialist health services.

Level 4:

→ For a standard-setting template for auditing the extent to which health services are family focused.

'The family in mental health work' – course summary

Aims

The aim of the course is to promote mental health professionals' capacity to use a transgenerational approach to family mental health. Course participants will acquire knowledge and skills in three areas:

1. Increased awareness of families' needs when parents have a mental illness.

2. How clinicians may use TFM to guide their family-focused practice.

3. An appreciation of key processes and tasks involved in integrating theory with practice to ensure sustainability and generalisation of learning to the service setting.

Figure 1: cross sectional components of TFM

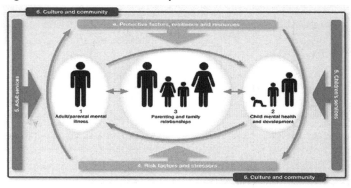

Figure 2: the six Domains

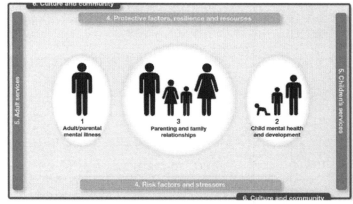

Figure 3: Ten arrows

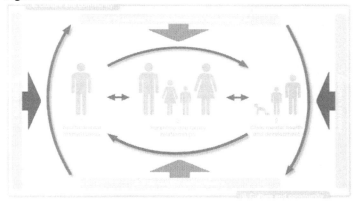

Figure 4: Lifespan and developmental perspective

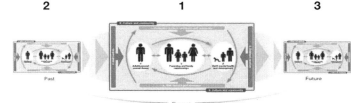

As well as conveying an understanding of the interplay between relationships and symptoms, the course also provides an approach to practice, thus ensuring integration of theoretical and practical perspectives.

Development and design

The development of the course was based upon situated learning theory (Vygotsky, 1978; Lave & Wenger, 1991) and evidence based practice (EBP). In order to ensure that the course meets health services skill requirements we incorporated relevant research, legislation and policy guidelines, user's and relatives' experiences, and clinical and pedagogical expertise. Given the relevance of partnership working, the reference group was established to underpin collaboration as a fundamental principle in both the course development and its delivery (Repper & Breeze, 2007; Norwegian Social and Health directorate, 2005).

A collaboration approach

The Norwegian development team (consisting of adviser, educators, researchers and clinicians) met on a regular basis and attended various conferences and presentations over a two-year period. The reference group attended presentations of TFM with Dr. Falkov and provided feedback to the development team on a regular basis. There was regular communication with Dr. Falkov, site visits, talks, workshops and recording lectures, as well as information about the development and use of TFM. The films are made available for students on the course's web-based learning platform. Dr. Anne Grant provided assistance with clinical case material from her research on TFM in Ireland (Grant, 2014).

Structure

The course capacity is 25 students and it is delivered over eight weeks (including three weeks to write the final exam). The intention is to also be able to offer the course in English for overseas, English-speaking students.

The course curriculum and content are available on the University College's web-based learning platform, which is structured according to situated learning requirements (Vygotsky, 1978; Lave & Wenger, 1991; Willis & Cifuentes, 2005; Herrington, 2015). It consists of lectures, seminars and workshops, tutorials, case studies, self-directed learning and group work. The site provides supplementary material via technology-enhanced learning, including videos, presentations, research-based case studies linked to TFM domains and associated questions, an online discussion forum, and shared assignments. The site also provides external resources such as online films, scientific and popular papers, laws and regulations, and tools for clinical/family work etc. Lectures are provided by user organisations from mental health and substance abuse, researchers, clinicians and academics.

Content

Content is comprehensive and is delivered within the structure of TFM (the six Domains), with an emphasis on a holistic understanding of family focus in mental health practices. Topics include:

→ Lived experience expertise, such as mental illness experienced by parents and their relatives, consequences for health, life situation, living conditions.

→ Consequences for children when a parent is mentally ill.

→ Relatives' and user's knowledge.

→ Research.

→ Psychological development including attachment and resilience in children.

→ Cultural and social issues in the family.

→ Collaboration between patients, relatives and health professionals.

→ Collaboration between the different health and social services.

→ Laws and regulations (specifically tied to competing interests and dilemmas regarding consent and confidentiality).

→ Ethical challenges and dilemmas.

Course requirements

Students are expected to undertake:

→ Written assignments describing a family based on TFM, and describing key areas of importance for an individual's/family's mental health.

→ Training using 'family conversations' with mutual reflection in groups.

→ A written, practical, reasoned, treatment programme for the family in a social and professional context with an emphasis on enablers/obstacles to family work in practice. This is presented at a seminar.

→ A written assignment that reflects their own experiences using TFM.

Learning outcomes

The students are expected to achieve a good general understanding of the impact of mental illness on various family members, and the benefits of family-focused practice. Furthermore, they should gain advanced knowledge about all TFM domains, particularly awareness of competing needs and interests across two or more generations and clinical dilemmas about family-focused practice in mental health. There is a strong emphasis on developing critical thinking skills in ethical, legal and professional dilemmas, as well as how family collaboration within mental health services can occur. Substantial effort is provided to illustrate interconnections between clinical work, research and education.

Knowledge to practice

The course emphasises the acquisition and use of skills related to family-focused practice. Considerable time is spent focusing on implications of the course learning objectives for clinical practice. The challenges and rewards of collaborative practice are discussed, written about and practiced. Talks from relatives and service users illustrate lived experience and lectures and learning materials place emphasis on practical and clinical implications of theoretical knowledge (from 'what' to 'how'). Students are encouraged to reflect on the impact of learning on themselves and their own experiences as individuals, family members and professionals. These approaches are delivered using the domains of TFM.

Student reflections of the utility of the course

An open dialogue evaluation of the course as a whole was undertaken and students also submitted written assignments, which included reflections on TFM and its utility. They stated:

→ that research cases could have been better incorporated into lectures

→ a wish for more information on sibling experiences within families

→ it would be useful to have more practice doing TFM role play.

They emphasised the international perspective, the breadth and depth of the required knowledge base on systems/ecological approach and the importance of exploring multiple perspectives (family, professional, mental health, legal and ethical) in family-focused practice. Managing possible conflicts of interest was also important.

The assignments were noted to be especially important, both in content and timing. The latter assisted with reflection and preparation for a broader appreciation and understanding. Small group work was rewarding, especially in discussing challenging and sensitive topics. Role play with reflecting teams was also a 'must' in students' opinions – essential to a fuller understanding of the potential of TFM. They were also supportive of course content being accessible on the web-based learning platform, which they found especially helpful with their final exam.

In summary, students stated that they had learnt a lot, were enthusiastic about using a family-focused practice approach, with ideas for practice change. They expressed that the course gave them hope for a change in their future practice.

Students' reflections on TFM

→ 'I have become more aware of all the research, which highlights the need for a family focus…'

→ '…it made a strong impression to reading and hearing stories from children who have been relatives and caregivers for their parents.'

→ 'I have also become aware of how important it is for a parent to get help to be a good parent and maintain contact with the child.'

→ 'It has previously been depressing to hear about how mental illness and problems are being "inherited" over the generations. That is why TFM and this approach was experienced as a bright spot in relation to preventing, early detection and the possibility of building on resources, look for resources and focus on resources.'

→ '…the model can be applied to such diverse areas; both on a superior level (theoretical and practical) and in clinical work in meeting with families.'

→ '…also suitable for teaching and can be understood by various professions … suitable to get a 'common language' and understanding.'

→ '…using TFM as a tool in specialist and community health care will probably enable a better use of resources, have a preventive effect, and help early identifying different challenges.'

Summary

Early experience in developing the inaugural Master's programme at Oslo and Akershus University College has demonstrated the feasibility of delivering a comprehensive course on family-focused practice using TFM. Based on informal feedback, it appears to have been well received and is acceptable to all participants. It seems to meet an important need for a comprehensive, understandable and practical approach to family-focused practice.

It is also pleasing to note that the current course is oversubscribed and there is now a waiting list. However, it will be important to undertake a more formal evaluation as part of continuous quality improvement for ongoing course refinement.

Ultimately, it remains to be seen whether the generalisation and sustainability of individual participants' family-focused practice occurs within teams and services and whether this really does make a positive difference to the lives of parents with mental illness and their relatives.

References

Beardslee WR, Versage EM, Gladstone TR (1998) Children of affectively ill parents: a review of the past 10 years. *Journal of the American Academy of Child and Adolescent Psychiatry* **37** (11) 1134–41.

Bird V (2010) Early intervention services, cognitive-behavioural therapy and family intervention in early psychosis: systematic review. *British Journal of Psychiatry* **197** (5) 350–356.

Ewertzon M, Cronqvist A, Lützén K & Andershed B (2012) A lonely life journey bordered with struggle: being a sibling of an individual with psychosis. *Issues in mental health nursing* **33** (3) 157–164.

Falkov A (2012) *The Family Model Handbook: an integrated approach to supporting mentally ill parents and their children*. Hove: Pavilion Publishing.

Falkov A (2015) Translating the family model into practice change. In: Reupert, Mayberry, Nicholson, Gopfert & Seeman. *Parental Psychiatric Disorder: Distressed Parents and Their Children*. 3rd Edition. Cambridge: Cambridge University Press.

Falkov A, Goodyear M, Hosman CM, Biebel K, Skogøy BE, Kowalenko N & Re E (2016) A systems approach to enhance global efforts to implement family-focused mental health interventions. *Child & Youth Services* 1–19.

Foster K, Maybery D, Reupert A, Gladstone B, Grant A, Ruud T & Kowalenko N (2016) Family-focused practice in mental health care: an integrative review. *Child & Youth Services* 1–27.

Grant A (2014). *Registered psychiatric nurses' practice with parents who have mental illness, their children and families, within general adult mental health services in Ireland*. A Thesis Submitted in partial fulfillment of the Requirements of Monash University for the Degree of Doctor of Philosophy. Melbourne: Monash University.

Herrington J (2015) Towards a new tradition of online instruction: using situated learning theory to design web-based units [online]. Available at: https://pdfs.semanticscholar.org/74ba/261a72ffa4002411d2bad33d6c4ee20e26bd.pdf (accessed July 2017).

Johansson A, Ewertzon M, Andershed B, Anderzen-Carlsson A, Nasic S & Ahlin A (2015) Health-related quality of life – from the perspective of mothers and fathers of adult children suffering from long-term mental disorders. *Archives of Psychiatric Nursing* **29** (3) 180–185.

Kletthagen Skundberg H (2015) *Everyday life of relatives of persons suffering from severe depression: experiences of health, burden, sense of coherence and encounters with psychiatric specialist health services*. Doctoral thesis. Karlstad University, Sweden.

Lave J & Wenger E (1991) Communities of practice: creating learning environments for educators. Cambridge University Press. P. 14. ISBN 9780521423748.

Maybery D & Reupert A (2009) Parental mental illness: a review of barriers and issues for working with families and children. *Journal of Psychiatric and Mental Health Nursing* **16** (9) 784–791.

Norwegian Directorate of Health (2010) *Children as relatives*. Circular IS-5/2010.

Norwegian Social and Health directorate (2005) *… and it will be better*.

National Strategy for Quality Improvement in social and health services (2005-2015) Guidelines IS1162, Oslo.

Okpokoro U, Adams CE & Sampson S (2014) Family intervention (brief) for schizophrenia. *Cochrane Database of Systematic Reviews* **5** (3) CD009802.

Repper J & Breeze J (2007) User and carer involvement in the training and education of health professionals: a review of the literature. *International Journal of Nursing Studies* **44** (3) 511–519.

Reupert A, Maybery D & Nicholson J (2015) Towards the development of a conceptual framework. In: A Reupert, D Maybery, J Nicholson, M Göpfert & MV Seeman (Eds) (2015) *Parental Psychiatric Disorder: Distressed parents and their families*. 3rd Edition. Cambridge University Press.

Reupert A, Maybery D, Nicholson J, Göpfert M & Seeman MV (Eds). (2015). *Parental Psychiatric Disorder: Distressed Parents and their Families*. 3rd Edition. Cambridge: Cambridge University Press.

Siegenthaler E, Munder T & Egger M (2012) Effect of preventive interventions in mentally ill parents on the mental health of the offspring: systematic review and meta-analysis. *Journal of the American Academy of Child & Adolescent Psychiatry* **51** (1) 8–17.

Smith M (2004) Parental mental health: disruptions to parenting and outcomes for children. Child & Family Social Work 9 3–11. doi:10.1111/j.1365-2206.2004.00312.x

Vygotsky L (1978) *Mind in Society*. London: Harvard University Press.

Weimand BM, Hedelin B, Sällström C & Hall-Lord ML (2010) Burden and health in relatives of persons with severe mental illness: a Norwegian cross-sectional study. *Issues in Mental Health Nursing* **31** (12) 804–815.

Weimand BM (2012) *Experiences and nursing support of relatives of persons with severe mental illness*. Doctoral thesis. Karlstad University, Sweden.

Weimand BM, Sällström C, Hall-Lord ML & Hedelin B (2013) Nurses' dilemmas concerning support of relatives in mental health care. *Nursing Ethics* **20** (3) p285–99.

Willis J & Cifuentes L (2005) Training teachers to integrate technology into the classroom curriculum: online versus face-to-face course delivery. *Journal of Technology and Teacher Education* **3** (1) p43–54.

Impacts and influences on mental health recovery, parenting and children's development and well-being

Do families with mental ill health have a 'voice'? Gatekeeping in health and social care research

Jennie Rose, Sarah Redsell and Jane Akister

Introduction

This paper is prompted by the authors' experience recruiting participants for a research project focused on preventing overweight during infancy (Proactive Assessment of Obesity during Infancy (Redsell et al, 2017). The research involved health visitors identifying potential participants during routine home visits to new parents. Although the protocol had clear inclusion and exclusion criteria relating to anxiety and depression, health visitors were reluctant to approach parents who they thought might have any mental health concerns. Acting as gatekeepers, they informally excluded these potential participants from the research.

The practice of researchers gaining access to participants via intermediaries was precipitated by the Data Protection Act (1998) (DPA), which specified that organisations need permission to pass on personal details to third parties. This led to the current situation in which research establishments are unable to directly contact people receiving care from health and social care organisations in order to recruit them into research projects. Consequently, it falls to client-facing professionals to identify and approach eligible participants, and to act as 'gatekeepers', deciding who has the opportunity to take part in research. Shortly after the DPA was introduced, Redsell & Cheater (2001) cautioned that it made research more vulnerable to recruitment bias and caused issues with external validity. This indeed seems to be the case, with reports of researchers experiencing difficulties with gatekeepers excluding people who are eligible for their study. 'Excluded' groups have included patients with depression (Hughes-Morley et al, 2015), people who are socially disadvantaged or socially excluded (Bonevski et al, 2014), ethnic minority communities (McAreavey & Das, 2013), potentially vulnerable pregnant women (Stuart et al, 2015), patients with cancer (e.g. Gurwitz et al, 2001) and looked-after children in a social care setting (Mezey et al, 2015).

While gatekeepers are trying to protect their clients, the result is that some vulnerable people do not have the opportunity to participate – they lose their voice. With an estimated quarter of people in England experiencing a mental health problem in any year, gatekeeper exclusion of families with mental ill health has the potential to affect the external validity and hence generalisability of research in health and social care. In this paper we explore some of the reasons behind gatekeeping, including whether research is a burden for a family, whether it might be detrimental for the vulnerable child, and whether the professionals feel exposed.

Gatekeepers believe that research is too much of a burden for the family

'… some of the families I already knew had mild depression … wouldn't respond well to participating, so yeah, I didn't ask them.' (Health Visitor, ProAsk study)

The notion that offering the choice to participate in research could have adverse effects on some families, even where they meet the study's inclusion criteria, implies that the gatekeeping professional is being overprotective. Drawing on our own experience of recruiting participants to the ProAsk study, we proposed that mothers with a diagnosis of postnatal depression should be excluded from the study. As the gatekeepers to potential parent participants, health visitors were consulted about the protocol and advised that the exclusion criteria relating to mental ill health should be broadened so that mothers with moderate post-natal depression or anxiety scores were also excluded. These criteria were approved by the NHS Research Ethics Committee. However, during recruitment it became apparent that some health visitors were excluding mothers with *any* mental health issue; their protectiveness led to a protocol deviation which made the study sample susceptible to bias in favour of parents with no reported mental health issues.

We argue that a protective bias may be operating across both health and social care research, and seems to be a particular cause for concern where there are mental health issues. A recent systematic review of depression trials concluded that clinician gatekeepers often showed a protective bias that impacted on the recruitment of participants (Hughes-Morley et al, 2015). Diggins (2016) attempted to recruit participants for research into parental mental health and child protection and found that social workers felt that participating in research would place unnecessary strain on the families. While ethical research demands that the interests of the most vulnerable in society are safeguarded, it also requires that the individual's right to make autonomous decisions is respected. Even if the intention is to protect, a decision by gatekeepers not to offer the opportunity to take part in research necessarily results in a loss of autonomy for that person and a shift towards paternalism.

Roberts and Kim (2014) found that the overprotectiveness shown by gatekeepers in trials involving patients with mental health issues such as depression, anxiety and schizophrenia is driven by a tendency to overestimate the vulnerabilities of these patients. Although motivated by protectiveness, it has serious implications. A gatekeeper's decision not to offer an opportunity for research participation to an eligible person suggests that in the professional's judgment the potential participant lacks capacity to make the decision for him or herself. The Mental Capacity Act (2005) makes it clear that it must be established (rather than assumed) that a person lacks capacity to make a given decision. This requirement is not satisfied where a gatekeeper decides not to offer a client or patient a particular research opportunity on the basis of their intuition about conditions and circumstances. There is, however, evidence that health care professionals who identify and approach patients with mental health issues about research participation often draw on their intuition regarding the person's vulnerability rather than a formal medical assessment (Witham et al, 2015). Such intuitions are highly susceptible to assumptions about how mental health status might affect decision-making abilities, and make recruitment to research susceptible to unconscious and unspoken biases that are difficult to scrutinise.

The assumption that people with mental ill health are particularly vulnerable to being overwhelmed by the demands of research also relies on the belief that research participation is burdensome. Reviewing the evidence of risks and benefits of research participation for people from populations defined as vulnerable, Alexander (2010) found 100 articles that reported positive outcomes from research participation by individuals from vulnerable populations, but only one reporting negative outcomes.

The benefits of using research participants from vulnerable populations include:

→ gaining new insights and information

→ feeling valued

→ a sense of altruism

→ social contact for the socially isolated, which brings the opportunity for associated psychological benefits

→ normalisation of their experience.

Alexander concludes that there is there is little evidence that research is especially harmful for individuals from vulnerable populations.

Research that seeks the views of people with depression, anxiety and schizophrenia who have taken part in clinical research supports this contention. Interviewed about their experiences of and attitudes towards research participation, they did not see themselves as more vulnerable than other participants and they valued being given the opportunity to take part (Roberts & Kim, 2014). Gatekeepers may be placing undue emphasis on the possible risks to their clients. In consequence, they may be both failing to recognise their

strengths and denying them the opportunity to experience the potential benefits from participating in research. Being constructed as 'helpless' by professionals risks reinforcing the loss of agency associated with depression. Effectively, gatekeeping silences patients denying choice and autonomy (Witham et al, 2015).

The problem with paternalistic gatekeeping to 'protect' the potential participant is that this silencing means they lose their voice, and services developed from research lack the vital contribution that these people can make.

Gatekeepers believe participating in research might be bad for the child

Research involving children may be particularly vulnerable to gatekeeping. Layers of gatekeepers, from ethics committees to professionals, parents, caregivers and teachers, control access to a potential child participant (Powell & Smith, 2009). It is the ethical responsibility of these gatekeepers to protect the child. But they also have a responsibility to promote the child's right to have their freely expressed views taken into account in matters that affect them (United Nations Convention on the Rights of the Child, Article 12). Like adults with mental health concerns, gatekeepers' perceptions of children as vulnerable and lacking competence to make decisions can result in overprotection, which limits their participation in research. This problem was articulated 20 years ago by Morrow and Richards (1996) and remains as pertinent today (Tromp & Vathorst, 2015). As Luchtenberg et al (2015) found, young people who had participated in clinical research subsequently revealed in interviews that they had wanted to take part in clinical trials before, but had not been offered the opportunity.

Where research has accessed the voices of young people it has proven important in service development and in the success of intervention. Diggins (2016) researched the added value of learning from success in parental mental health and child welfare work and reported: 'Young carers were proud of the role they undertook in their family and some viewed caring as a positive contributory factor to their own development' (Diggins, 2016, p100). Diggins also reports that children say they hide their own difficulties from their parents because they do not want to make them feel 'more guilty' and they are worried that services might intervene and separate them. Exploring the views of children and parents enables a picture to be developed of what the children feel contributes to success, including the nature of their relationships with helping professionals. Without hearing the voice of the child, assumptions are made about what they might contribute.

Professionals may feel exposed by the research

Health and social care professionals working in community settings practice in unsupervised contexts. In the space provided by professional autonomy it is difficult to make clinical judgements accountable (Grimen, 2009). As gatekeepers regulate access to potential research participants they may select participants that protect their own interests and activities (Emmel et al, 2007). Witham et al (2015) discuss gatekeepers' concerns for themselves as the main reason for not approaching potential participants with mental ill health.

Potential risks to gatekeepers include:

→ harm to the gatekeeper or associates

→ uninvited interference

→ being misrepresented

→ legal consequences.

(Clark, 2010)

Wolff (2004) suggests that a researcher's failure to gain access to participants is as illuminating about the field under study as their successes. Unsuccessful or problematic field negotiations should not necessarily be written off as failure at the personal level, nor a problem of relations, but rather seen as systemic responses to the threat of disruption. There is a clear need for researchers to develop relationships with gatekeepers so the perceived risk and uncertainty introduced by research becomes an opportunity for development and improved practice. Researchers need to understand and directly address the gatekeeper's concerns about introducing research to service users perceived too vulnerable to be asked. The negative stereotypes of research as burdensome and threatening could be challenged by researchers highlighting the evidence of the benefits for participants, and, for non-participants, the benefits of simply being offered the choice. At the same time, researchers should not shy away from sharing with client-facing professionals the serious implications of gatekeeping for equality and social justice.

Why is representative research important?

If research is not representative we may draw the wrong conclusions and develop poor policy. This can occur through biased or small samples. The actions of gatekeepers may result in biases into recruitment to research (Preston et al, 2016). This is problematic for both quantitative and qualitative research. Quantitative research seeks to study a representative sample of the population so that the results can be generalised to the wider population. If the sample is not representative the safety and effectiveness of new treatments and interventions cannot be demonstrated on important sub-groups of the population (Rugkåsa & Canvin, 2011). Within qualitative research, gatekeepers can exert an important influence over the voice of the more vulnerable participants, which influences the meanings and social understanding that qualitative research can gain. The subgroups who are not represented are often those whose experiences will be most valuable to the qualitative researcher.

It is of particular concern if people with the highest burden of illness are excluded from research. People with more than one health concern are one such group. There is evidence that gatekeepers may choose not to offer research opportunities to eligible participants because the patient has co-morbidities (Jenkinson et al, 2014). To illustrate this problem, even when research is designed to meet a particular and pressing need in patients with both physical and mental ill health, the additional burden of research was perceived by health care professionals as an overwhelming threat (Witham et al, 2015). Mental health disorders, particularly depression, are more prevalent in people with increasing numbers of physical disorders. Gatekeeping on the grounds of physical and mental health co-morbidity therefore poses a serious threat to the representativeness of research and presents a barrier to understanding how people with the highest burden of illness experience their predicaments.

There is also evidence that gatekeepers restrict access to research participation by people from lower socio-economic groups (Bonevski et al, 2014). Since common health disorders are more prevalent in socially disadvantaged populations (Fryers et al, 2003) gatekeeping on the basis of social groups hinders the development of an evidence base that could deliver interventions and policies that reduce health inequalities.

The problems of representativeness are compounded by the use of secondary data and meta-analysis, where data sets are combined and re-analysed to establish the validity of the findings. Despite techniques to maximise representativeness, some sub-populations remain underrepresented (Frederick et al, 2012). Once excluded, groups are excluded again. This is important because such data can be influential for guidelines and policy; systematic reviews are seen by some as the pinnacle of evidence-based practice.

Conclusion

The task of research is to further our understanding and to translate these findings into policy and practice. We need to understand what contributes to poor mental and physical health and we need insights into the experiences of children in troubled families. To promote parental mental health and child welfare we need to research those at risk and have to rely on gatekeepers to access these populations. There are risks in exposing people to research, and gatekeepers need to be mindful of this, but at the same time it is vital that these people have a voice and that we are able to develop policy and practice that reflects their lived experience. By highlighting some of the reasons behind gatekeeping and some of its effects, we hope to equip and encourage researchers to engage with gatekeepers and promote the potential benefits of research participation for people from vulnerable and marginalised populations.

References

Alexander SJ (2010) As long as it helps somebody: why vulnerable people participate in research. *International Journal of Palliative Nursing* **16** (4) 174–9.

Bonevski B, Randell M, Paul C, Chapman K, Twyman L, Bryant J, Brozek I & Hughes C (2014) Reaching the hard-to-reach: a systematic review of strategies for improving health and medical research with socially disadvantaged groups. *BMC Medical Research Methodology* **14** (1) 42.

Clark T (2010) Gaining and maintaining access: exploring the mechanisms that support and challenge the relationship between gatekeepers and researchers. *Qualitative Social Work* **10** (4) 485–502.

Diggins M (2016) The added value of learning from success in parental mental health and child welfare work. *Parental Mental Health and Child Welfare Work* **1** 97–106.

Emmel N, Hughes K, Greenhalgh J & Sales A (2007) Accessing socially excluded people: trust and the gatekeeper in the researcher-participant relationship. *Sociological Research Online* **12** (2). Available at: http://www.socresonline.org.uk/12/2/emmel.html (accessed July 2016).

Frederick K, Barnard-Brak L & Sulak T (2012) Under representation in nationally representative secondary data. *International Journal of Research and Method in Education* **35** (1) 31-40.

Fryers T, Melzer D & Jenkins R (2003) Social inequalities and the common mental disorders. *Social Psychiatry and Psychiatric Epidemiology* **38** (5) 229–237.

Grimen H (2009) Power, trust, and risk: some reflections on an absent issue. *Medical Anthropology Quarterly* **23** (1) 16–33.

Gurwitz JH, Guadagnoli E, Landrum MB, Silliman RA, Wolf R & Weeks JC (2001) The treating physician as active gatekeeper in the recruitment of research subjects. *Medical Care* **39** (12) 1339–1344.

Hughes-Morley A, Young B, Waheed W, Small N & Bower P (2015) Factors affecting recruitment into depression trials: systematic review, meta-synthesis and conceptual framework. *Journal of Affective Disorders* **172** 274–290.

Jenkinson CE, Winder RE, Sugg HVR, Roberts MJ, Ridgway N, Kuyken W, Wiles N, Kessler D & Campbell J (2014) Why do GPs exclude patients from participating in research? An exploration of adherence to and divergence from trial criteria. *Family Practice* **31** (3) 364–70.

Luchtenberg M, Maeckelberghe E, Locock L, Powell L. & Verhagen AAE (2015) Young People's Experiences of participation in clinical trials: reasons for taking part. *The American Journal of Bioethics* **15** (11) 3–13.

McAreavey R & Das C (2013) A delicate balancing act: negotiating with gatekeepers for ethical research when researching minority communities. *International Journal of Qualitative Methods* **12** (1) 113–131.

McManus S, Meltzer H, Brugha T, Bebbington P & Jenkins R (2009) *Adult Psychiatric Morbidity in England 2007: Results of a household survey* [online]. Available at: http://www.hscic.gov.uk/pubs/psychiatricmorbidity07 (accessed 9 July 2016).

Mezey G, Robinson F, Campbell R, Gillard S, Macdonald G, Meyer D, Bonell C & White, S (2015) Challenges to undertaking randomised trials with looked after children in social care settings. *Trials* **16** (1) 1–15.

Morrow V & Richards M (1996) The ethics of social research with children: an overview. *Children and Society* **10** (2) 90-105.

Powell MA & Smith AB (2009) Children's Participation Rights in Research. *Childhood* **16** (1) 124–142.

Preston NJ, Farquhar MC, Walshe CE, Stevinson C, Ewing G, Calman LA, Burden S, Brown Wilson C, Hopkinson JB & Todd C (2016) *Strategies Designed to Help Healthcare Professionals to Recruit Participants to Research Studies. Cochrane Database of Systematic Reviews* [online]. Available at: http://onlinelibrary.wiley.com/doi/10.1002/14651858.MR000036.pub2/pdf (accessed July 2016).

Redsell SA & Cheater FM (2001) The Data Protection Act (1998): implications for health researchers. *Journal of Advanced Nursing* **35** (4) 508-513.

Redsell SA, Rose J, Weng S, Ablewhite J, Swift JA, Siriwardena AN, Nathan D, Wharrad HJ, Atkinson P, Watson P, McMaster F, Lakshman R & Glazebrook C (2017) Digital technology to facilitate Proactive Assessment of Obesity Risk during Infancy (ProAsk): a feasibility study. BMJ Open 2017;7:e017694. doi: 10.1136/bmjopen-2017-017694.

Roberts LW & Kim JP (2014) Giving voice to study volunteers: comparing views of mentally ill, physically ill, and healthy protocol participants on ethical aspects of clinical research. *Journal of Psychiatric Research* **56** 90–7.

Rugkåsa J & Canvin K (2011) Researching mental health in minority ethnic communities: reflections on recruitment. *Qualitative Health Research* **21** (1) 132–143.

Scourfield P (2012) Defenders against threats or enablers of opportunities: the screening role played by gatekeepers in researching older people in care homes. *The Qualitative Report* **17** (14) 1–17.

Stuart J, Barnes J, Spiby H & Elbourne D (2015) Understanding barriers to involving community midwives in identifying research participants; experience of the first steps randomised controlled trial. *Midwifery* **31** (8) 779–786.

Tromp K & Vathorst SVD (2015) Gatekeeping by professionals in recruitment of pediatric research participants: Indeed an undesirable practice. *The American Journal of Bioethics* **15** (11) 30–32.

Witham G, Beddow A & Haigh C (2015) Reflections on access: too vulnerable to research? *Journal of Research in Nursing* **20** (1) 28–37.

Wolff S (2004) Ways into the field and their variants. In: U Flick, RV Kardoff and I Steinke (Eds) *A Companion to Qualitative Research* (pp195–202). London: Sage.

Grandparents as primary caregivers for their grandchildren when parents have a mental illness

Vicki Cowling

Introduction

In many parts of the world, grandparents are increasingly becoming primary caregivers for their grandchildren (Cuddeback, 2004; Dunne & Kettler, 2008; Fuller-Thomson, 2005). Although there are many reasons for this, mental illness and substance use problems experienced by parents are contributory. For reasons related to fear of stigma, adherence to cultural tradition, or concern about the involvement of statutory authorities, care giving by grandparents remains partly invisible (House of Representatives Standing Committee on Family, Community, Housing and Youth, 2009; Horner et al, 2007). Further, some grandparents may not openly acknowledge their caregiving role.

Prevalence of grandparents raising grandchildren

In Australia, grandparents provide primary care for children aged between 0-17 years in 16,000 families (Australian Bureau of Statistics, 2011). In the United States, in 2009, 7.8 million children (11% of all children) lived with at least one grandparent (Kreider, & Ellis, 2011), with numbers increasing. Numbers are also increasing in England and Wales (Glaser et al, 2013). The increasing prevalence of grandparent care derives from two trends – parental incapacity and a preference for kinship care by mandated welfare authorities and families themselves.

The prevalence of grandparental care is likely to be higher than reported for the reasons cited above, and in many cultures grandparents expect to look after their grandchildren and therefore do not self-identify as carers. This is true for families from indigenous backgrounds in Australia (Brennan et al, 2013), Canada (Fuller-Thomson, 2005), and for Hispanic and African Americans in the US (Jimenez, 2002).

A further hidden group are those grandparents who become parents to their grandchildren when parents have a mental illness (Cowling et al, 2015). The use of 'parent' in this context relies on a social definition of being a parent, which recognises that parenting involves duties, roles and responsibilities, and is not limited to a relationship based on biology (Sullivan, 2001).

Why do grandparents become primary carers for their grandchildren?

Where intervention and support are required from services, it is important to understand the personal motivation of grandparents in becoming carers for their grandchildren in order to plan effective interventions with them.

Commonly cited reasons for grandparents raising their grandchildren include physical or mental illness and disability of the parents, incarceration, death, military service, family breakdown, or child abuse and neglect on the part of a parent. Grandparents who step in to become carers for their grandchildren often do so as they will not contemplate any alternative, as were the experiences of Jennifer (2008) and Harriet (2008) presented below, or they may feel a family obligation and responsibility. Of course, grandparents are also willing to become primary caregivers for their grandchildren because they love and are attached to them.

The impact on grandparents of becoming parents to their grandchildren

Grandparents who become carers may be impacted in various ways, some of which distinguish them from other providers of out-of-home care. At short notice, or sometimes with virtually no notice, they are asked to or feel obliged to become the full-time carer to their grandchild/ren. In taking up this role, grandparents may experience loss at suddenly having to relinquish whatever their life meant at the time, such as working, travelling or recreational activities, and they may experience grief that their son or daughter's illness has limited their capacity to parent their children themselves. Self-reflection about their own parenting occurs for some, and may be a source of profound and ongoing sadness.

The physical, mental, social and financial well-being of grandparents may be affected when they assume the role of 'grandparent as parent'. Factors influencing these outcomes include the grandparent's age and gender, characteristics of the child, and the health and the role of the child's parent. Health related quality of life among grandparent carers varies but is significantly below US population means (Neely-Barnes et al, 2010). In one large study, over 55% of grandparent carers reported three or more health problems, and 45% took five or more medications (Kolomer, 2009). Before taking on the task of caring for grandchildren, custodial grandparents may already be suffering from physical and emotional problems, many of them associated with advancing age (Neely-Barnes et al, 2010). Young, middle-aged and elderly grandparents will have different additional responsibilities and different frailties, and will therefore be differently affected (Sands & Goldberg-Glen, 2000).

Some differences in health risks have been reported between grandfathers and grandmothers who raise grandchildren. When compared to grandmothers, the grandfathers in one small study scored lower on life satisfaction, emotional health and physical health. They were, however, older than the grandmothers (Okagbue-Reaves, 2005).

The number, age, temperament and experiences of the children is important as a possible contributor to extra stressors for grandparents. An infant requiring full-time care, having unsettled sleep and childhood infections may be more demanding than a child attending school each day.

The relationship grandparents have with their grandchildren will be influenced by the age of the children. A grandparent caring for a grandchild of any age may feel out of touch with current parenting practices, although becoming parent to an infant grandchild gives the grandparent the opportunity to have a parenting style that is their own. Becoming a grandparent to older children who verbally and behaviourally may overtly express distress at being taken from their parent, requires understanding and patience on the part of the grandparent.

The nature, severity and stability of the mental illness of the grandchild's parent will be critical in determining grandparental stress levels. There may be disagreement between parent and grandparent and health may suffer in the context of a contentious atmosphere, particularly when the parent has involuntarily relinquished care of their child (Grinstead et al, 2003).

Securing suitable housing may be a problem for grandparents as children may not be allowed to reside in senior housing units, and appropriate housing may be unaffordable (Fuller-Thompson & Minkler, 2003). In addition, taking on the caregiver role will lead to additional daily living expenses, and may at the same time also lead to a decrease in income if the grandparent has to cut back on employment. While grandparents may be entitled to public assistance, some grandparents choose not to seek this support.

Grandparents may become marginalised and isolated within their communities because they do not have time to pursue their activities and interests, or do not have the financial means to do so. Their peers may not welcome young children at social gatherings, and accessing and paying for babysitting may not be possible. Accompanying children to school, helping with homework, and taking children to extracurricular activities may be tiring and difficult experiences for grandparents. There may also be more than one child involved, with individual behaviours and temperaments, which increases the difficulty of the task.

As kinship carers, grandparents receive fewer agency-based supports than non-kin caregivers such as foster parents. Inadequate support may result in depression for grandparent carers (Musil et al, 2009).

Brennan et al's (2013) survey of 335 reported that the impact of grandparent care included financial disadvantage, the need to reduce working hours or cease working altogether, or the need to change housing arrangements. These changes often involved significant costs and experiences of social isolation and disrupted friendships. The grandparents also reported that more than 80% of the grandchildren had emotional or behavioural problems, with 50% having physical problems.

Approximately two thirds of the grandparents participated in a support group (Brennan et al, 2013). These groups have been found to help grandparents learn from one another about legal rights and financial entitlements, as well as giving them access to social and psychological support (Gerard et al, 2006). While support groups reduce stress and isolation, few have been formally evaluated, so evidence of lasting change is lacking (Blustein et al, 2004).

The grandparents surveyed by Brennan et al (2013) also accessed other sources of information and support, such as respite care, childcare and information on helping with schoolwork. However, they reported that finding support was difficult and required a lot of knowledge and effort on their part. They lacked understanding about their eligibility and identified parenting gaps. One grandmother explained, 'My boys are growing up with one elderly grandma. They need regular contact with good male role models' (Brennan et al, 2013, p125).

The lower the family cohesion the greater the psychological anxiety experienced by grandparents, 'which is consistent with the fact that grandparents become surrogate parents as a consequence of breakdown in the family system' (Sands & Goldberg-Glen, 2000, p101). Further, grandmothers who reported fewer resources, less social support and poorer physical health tended to experience higher levels of psychological distress (Kelley et al, 2000). Becoming a grandparent carer is a significant change of role and may impact on family relationships. Grandparents may experience relationship difficulties with each other and even separation and divorce because of the demands of caring for grandchildren, the loss of time together, and the 'shattering of their plans for the future' (Fitzpatrick & Reeve, 2003, p57).

Other children and adult offspring may be angry that their sibling is not taking responsibility for their own children, and grandparents may experience loss of contact with family members including their other grandchildren. The change in role from 'grandparent' to 'parent' may lead to grandparents mourning the loss of a normal grandparent relationship with the grandchildren in their care.

For many grandparents, their relationship with their grandchildren is maintained in the knowledge they themselves are growing older, with concerns about the possibility of ill health and confronting their own mortality. Related to this for some is the cost of medications they need as 'prescriptions eat into our wages' (Fitzpatrick & Reeve, 2003, p57).

Factors associated with well-being in grandparents who are parenting their grandchildren

Grandparenting in older age can be associated with personal well-being, an adaptive stance toward disruptive behaviour and positive feelings toward the grandchild (Hayslip *et al*, 2006). In a sample of 12,872 grandparents (not all of them custodial) aged 50 to 80 from the US-based Health and Retirement Study, no evidence was found for widespread negative effects on caregiving grandparents' health and health behaviour. The investigators concluded that health disadvantages described in the literature may arise from grandparents' prior characteristics, such as resourcefulness (Musil *et al*, 2009), and not as a direct consequence of providing care (Hughes *et al*, 2007). High levels of informal and community resources and enhanced resilience within families were shown to improve well-being (Sands *et al*, 2005).

Culture is an important variable – for example, being a grandparent carer is not unusual in the Black community and the stresses and strains of custodial grandparenthood may therefore be lessened (Minkler & Fuller-Thomson, 2005). In comparison to Caucasian Americans, African American grandmothers were found to report less loneliness and more social support, which can be attributed to the closeness of African American families (Kohn & Smith, 2006).

Experiences of two grandmothers raising their grandchildren when their parents had a mental illness

The following accounts show how taking on the parenting role by grandparents may come about, and they look at the impact on Jennifer and Harriet respectively. The first-person account by Jennifer (2008) describes the events that led to her becoming the full-time carer for her grandchildren, and the involvement of various services and her family, which enabled her to continue. Harriet (2008) changed her place of living to care for her grandson and travelled considerable distances to ensure he maintained connection with his mother. All names are pseudonyms and were chosen by the authors.

Jennifer: ... *No question*

I was on holiday in New South Wales in 2003 when I got a call from one of Margaret's friends asking me to get home as soon as possible (Margaret is my youngest child, and only daughter). At the time, Margaret's former housemate, James, and my youngest son, John, were living with me not far from Margaret's flat.

The boys tried to explain Margaret's behaviour to me, and it was exceedingly embarrassing for both of them. She claimed 'voodoo' people were attacking her, and telling her that the boys were both evil, and she was screaming this out for the whole neighbourhood to hear. The extent of her departure from reality included accusations that both James and John were 'psychically raping her'. When she confronted me the first time after I arrived home, she was so angry when I didn't believe her, she seized a hatchet and chased me around the back yard, until I went inside and called the police. This was the beginning of her treatment for psychotic episodes, as she went to the Royal Adelaide Hospital (RAH) and thence to a ward in the psychiatric hospital. She was eventually sent to a hostel.

After she was released from there, she rented a Housing Trust flat where she met her husband. She fell pregnant and they were married in March, 2004. She seemed reasonably well during the pregnancy and Jake arrived in October that year.

During this time she was on medication and being looked after by a community mental health team. Although she still had delusions about voodoo, she seemed to be better most of the time. However, there were several episodes when she would phone me to come and help her as she was 'being attacked'. Her husband was becoming less and less patient with her illness, and at the time I sympathised with him.

Jake was a good baby and seemed to thrive. However, as I didn't get on well with his father I didn't spend as much time with him as I would have, in retrospect, had I been aware of the facts. These issues included his father's jealousy of Margaret's time taken up with Jake, his method of discipline (yelling and shutting him in his room), Margaret's lack of quality time with Jake (DVDs in preference to teaching toys), her lack of motivation to train him, and the haphazard way in which she fed him.

By this time, only my eldest son, Rick, was living with me. When Margaret told us she was expecting a second child we were both worried as we didn't know how she could cope with two if the illness had not shown any further improvement.

Shortly before Susanna was born, Jake's father hit him and then Margaret. As a result of this, I took Margaret to our local police station and Jake's father was picked up, charged and bailed on condition that he goes nowhere near any of us. At this time, the case has not been heard due to continuous deferrals. The following week Margaret went to hospital and Susanna was born in August 2007.

Jake came to stay with Rick and me while Margaret was in hospital, and it became immediately apparent that he had many issues which would need to be addressed – including toilet training, weaning from bottle (he was still having three per day), and weaning from jars of baby food. He had frequent disturbed nights but was able to go to sleep again after much reassurance.

Margaret and Susanna went home after six days and I stayed with her for the first two nights, with Jake back in his own bed. Observing that her leg was swollen, I insisted she get an appointment with her GP. We went the next day, and after radiology she was rushed back into hospital with a deep vein thrombosis (DVT). Jake came home with me again. After about 10 days, I was called in by the hospital to have a meeting with people from various agencies to discuss Margaret's inability to care for Susanna. At the time I felt that, with the underlying mental illness, the domestic violence, having a baby, DVT and being separated from Jake, she had plenty of valid reasons for her to 'lose the plot'. She seemed to think that she was a danger to all the babies in the hospital, believing they were being attacked through her. This was her explanation for the babies' crying.

So Susanna came home with me at 14 days old, and Margaret was sent to the RAH psychiatric ward while waiting for a bed in Helen Mayo House (HMH), the specialised mother-baby unit. Jake was still unsettled and having his second home 'invaded' by the baby was a further challenge for him. In due course, a bed was found for Margaret and Susanna at HMH, and Jake and I went into the 'visiting' stage. By this time, he seemed quite settled into coming 'home' to my house and not his own.

Unfortunately, Margaret was not able to respond to treatment in HMH or improve her care of Susanna, and on Jake's birthday we brought the baby home again. At this stage,

Margaret went back into another ward of the psychiatric hospital where a drastic medication change was tried: clozapine, which is very strong. It became apparent fairly soon that the drug was making a difference, and for the first time her 'voices' were fading. When the staff thought she was ready, she went back to HMH with Susanna for another trial. Finally (and sadly on her own birthday), it was agreed that although the clozapine was working for her, it did mean that she was not in a position to care for the children. After a further meeting with agencies (mental health and child protection), both children were placed in my care.

Jake's lack of language development had become painfully obvious when I compared his talking (one to two words at a time) with another three year old at HMH. An assessment by child health services revealed that although he was a bright, intelligent child, his language and behavioural development was quite limited – in some instances he rated as a one to two year old.

We commenced visits to child and adolescent mental health services (CAMHS) for speech and behavioural therapy. Jake had been going to childcare three days a week since he had come to live with me. His social skills had improved immensely but he still occasionally showed aggressive signs. We have never been able to leave him in the same room with Susanna without one of us present, for fear he may act aggressively toward her.

However, with time, and the stability and routine that are established, Jake has developed his lovely sunny nature (albeit very mischievous) and he appears to love Susanna, and not consider her the rival he at first thought. As this sibling behaviour is to be expected in general, the occasional posturing to take attention away from the baby is seen as quite normal. He is popular at childcare and his language skills are coming along very well. He now completes sentences, and although he has not caught up, I have no doubt that he will.

Life for me has changed, it would seem forever. I had come to Adelaide to escape my children, and now three of them live here, and I have two small grandchildren to raise. I am 63 years old. When Jake is ten, I will be 70. Margaret's illness had put some strain on my available free time, especially once she became pregnant with Susanna. But that was as nothing compared to the way things are at present.

When the question of care of the children was first mooted, my (and my son's) only reaction was that there was, indeed, no question. Foster care was and is not an option. The children's welfare is currently officially in the hands of the State Minister for Families and Communities, and I am primary carer. There is very little free time. Jake is currently going through the 'terrible twos'. He pushes most of my buttons, most of the time (told you he was smart!).

I no longer have a place to go to in my home that is mine. Susanna shares my bedroom, Jake shares my office. When it becomes possible, they will share the ex-office and I will move my desk and computer into my bedroom. At the moment that won't work because Jake could climb into Susanna's cot and wake her up at any time. My ex-lounge is the playroom with toys scattered all over.

I am coping. It does seem some days that we are slowly getting used to the huge changes. I am so lucky that my son is here to relieve the pressure and afford me windows of time out, but these are fraught with worry until I get home and see that all is well. My child protection services contact person is organising respite care for me, and I have agreed at last because I can't afford to go under. I resisted at first because I did not want Jake's routine to be changed yet again. (Apart from two or three short terms with her mother, Susanna has been with me for most of her six months of life.)

Getting along with Margaret (who is now home at her house) is another problem. We have to work with access visits, which at the moment are mostly at my house. When she doesn't do the right thing in this respect I feel very resentful even though I know I shouldn't, because it is the illness and not the person.

Helen Mayo House, child protection, child health, CAMHS, various care organisations, my own GP, my son and my friends all support me. I feel really lucky that there are so many people who care, including staff of much maligned government agencies. Helen Mayo House has been truly wonderful, keeping contact with me and providing assessment of Susanna long after she left there. They are always ready to help if I ring for advice.

Life has changed indeed, but after an easier day with Jake, including more cuddles than he used to give, and feeding Susanna (world's most perfect baby), I know that we are doing what we have to, and want to, which begs the question: how do mentally ill mothers and their children cope if they do not have the same support?

Harriet: The experience of a grandmother raising Sam, her grandson, from infancy

If there is one day in my life that I will remember above all others, it is 3rd November, 1993. I was preparing a lunch party for family and close friends to celebrate my mother's 80th birthday. My 16-year-old son and his girlfriend arrived before the guests, and announced that they were to be parents. I kept this news to myself and managed to host a lovely day.

My son had had a difficult few years and was living with other young people in a house close to home. I suspected they were using drugs but I had no idea to what extent. My son's girlfriend had run away from home when she was 12 and had little contact with her mother. Both had been raised in homes without a father and I was well aware of the disadvantages this can have in regard to respect for authority and discipline. My son's girlfriend often behaved erratically, and I was informed shortly before my grandson's birth that she had been previously diagnosed with schizophrenia and had a history of hospitalization and treatment.

They were just 17 when Sam was born prematurely and his mother had already moved back to where she grew up and was being helped by her mother and family. Most weekends I travelled some distance so that I could see Sam and help out where possible. My son commuted at weekends as he was still studying in Sydney.

Sam's mother was given a Department of Housing flat that was very comfortable and gave the family stability. Within a year, all had turned to grief. She had met someone else and my son, who adored his little boy, was told to go.

I bought a house in Newcastle, New South Wales, as a place for my son to live and to have his visits with Sam. My son was very capable with Sam and was spending more and more time with him. Within a year Sam's mother had abandoned him and gone to Queensland where she was arrested and admitted to a psychiatric hospital.

Sam was two when I took him to Queensland for his mother's birthday and a pre-Christmas visit. We stayed for a week in a motel and visited twice each day. Sam loved seeing his mother, and one of our saddest days was the final goodbye, and watching him waving to her as we left. Sam remembers this visit and I suspect that it is one of his earliest memories. My son obtained full custody of Sam and I moved to Newcastle to live with them.

At about this time I realised that my son was using heroin. The home situation became very volatile and he moved into his own place nearby. In spite of this my son was very capable and a good parent and I supported him having Sam to stay often.

I decided to stop working but found the transition easy as I threw myself into renovating the house and doing the garden. I had just turned 50 and I missed my friends and work mates but kept in touch by phone. Sam spent a few days each week at Family Day Care commencing when he was about two and a half, and he thrived on the contact with other children. He then attended pre-school, before starting school. He was a very happy little boy and rarely threw a tantrum or cried. I always encouraged his friends to visit and stay over and I made good friends with the young parents of these children. We also had lots of children living in our street and his early years were full of games and good company. Because I didn't work I was able to attend most school functions and be more involved with sporting activities. I was not able to do this when my son was at school and I realised what we had both missed out on. Sam and I have had lots of adventures and holidays away together.

Sam's mother has spent long periods of time in institutions and it is unlikely that she will recover. When Sam sees her she is never able to fully engage or focus on him. She rarely hugs him or kisses him goodbye. He worries about her safety when she is not in a hospital being cared for, and I am concerned about his emotional well-being as I have rarely seen him cry. Sometimes I just wish he would break down and let it all out but he silently keeps his feelings to himself. I have consulted a number of child social workers who tell me that he does open up more with them so I am grateful for their help and we will continue to consult them. I know he would dearly have loved to have his mother look after him. I could never replace her and I haven't tried to. I have a close relationship with her and do all I can to make her life easier and help Sam stay in contact. My family and close friends have criticised me for allowing this contact for the negative effects it has on him, but my argument is that, for better or worse, she is his mother and we have to deal with that reality – I know that when he is older he will want to be her protector and help her all he can. This is beginning to be evident now.

Being 'mother' to my grandchild is quite a different experience to that of raising my son. I have more patience, wisdom, tolerance and time. I enjoy the routine and I love having the time to cook more interesting meals, look after clothing more carefully and do mundane tasks at my leisure. Raising my son was very much done in the fast lane and I missed so many of the little pleasures.

The years are racing by and now that Sam is a teenager I am experiencing different emotions. I sometimes feel resentful when he displays teenage selfishness and is rude to me. He wants more independence and freedom to hang out with his friends and I am enjoying having more time to myself to enjoy time with my friends, and to care for my elderly mother and aunt.

Over the years I have had moments when I've resented my loss of freedom and felt that I did not choose the path I am on, but the things I have missed out on are superficial and I've had great pleasure and satisfaction from caring for my only grandchild. Naturally, I have fears for Sam's future and worry about peer pressure, drugs and alcohol and the effect his parents' drug problems have had on him. He is very close to his father who is finally doing well and studying. I hope that by directing Sam into healthy teenage pursuits he will continue to develop into a happy young man with good values and a positive self-identity. That would be all the reward I need for any sacrifices I have made.

Life rarely goes to plan and I feel very pleased with myself that I have met the challenge with love, acceptance, optimism and energy. I look forward to the coming years and know that there will be ups and downs, but I know that with good health I will continue to enjoy the ride.

Practice implications

Grandparents who are parenting their grandchildren face a lack of information about services and financial supports, a general insensitivity to their situation, stereotyping, and a lack of advocacy on their behalf (Hayslip & Kaminski, 2005). Practitioners can assist grandparents by using an ecological assessment framework that includes an understanding of the impact of stigma, assessment of risk and protective factors, and assessment of family and individual resources such as housing, finance, legal issues, marital and social relationships, and loss and grief (Cowling et al, 2010).

Implicit in completing assessments and planning interventions with grandparents is the need for effective co-ordination and communication between providers who have a professional role with the child and with the parent: that is, a family-focused formulation and intervention plan is needed.

Interventions in consultation with grandparents and co-ordination among service providers might include the following:

→ Counsel grandparents to support them in the transition from the role of grandparent to their parenting role, including managing anxiety about their new responsibilities and feelings of resentment and guilt they may have about the parent (their own daughter or son) being unable to care for their children.

→ Provide information about child development, particularly children's emotional needs at different ages, acknowledging also that the child is adjusting to separation from his/her parent.

→ Provide psycho-education about mental illness symptoms and treatment and how they may affect the child's parent, and assist grandparents to understand how the child's parent is experiencing the loss of their parental role.

→ Facilitate family counseling to enhance resilience through shared understanding of the changes for the family, including experiences of loss and grief.

→ Link grandparents to social support groups for psychological and moral support, information about legal rights, and processes for negotiating with government departments. Link them to available neighbourhood groups and online groups.

→ Implement a multimodal intervention program that decreases stress and improves health and social support.

→ Reduce the invisibility of grandparents' experience by educating service providers such as health and welfare practitioners, professionals, teachers and government officers about the role of grandparents as primary carers, and the entitlements of grandparents as carers.

(Cowling *et al*, 2010)

Grandparents are increasingly taking up the role of parent with their grandchildren for multiple reasons, impacting on their health and their social and financial situations. This chapter has aimed to increase understanding of the experiences of grandparents who are parenting their grandchildren when parents have a mental illness, and it has given personal accounts of Jennifer and Harriet, two grandparents with direct experience. Information about the prevalence of grandparents who are primary caregivers, effects on their health and well-being, and the complexities involved, provide context for these accounts. When working with grandparents, a family-focused approach is preferable with individual assessment and intervention plans included in the plans. Communication and co-ordination among services and between services and grandparents and families is essential to facilitate their participation in planning and decision making.

Acknowledgements:

Jennifer and Harriet gave their written permission for their previously published chapters to be included.

This chapter has drawn from the following:

Cowling V (2016) *Support for children and families living with a family member with mental illness*. Unpublished PhD thesis, The University of Newcastle, New South Wales, Australia.

Cowling V, Seeman MV & Göpfert M (2015) Grandparents as primary caregivers. In: A Reupert, D Maybery, J Nicholson, MV Seeman & M Göpfert (Eds) *Parental psychiatric disorder: Distressed parents and their families 3rd Ed* (pp 248–258). Cambridge: Cambridge University Press.

References

Australian Bureau of Statistics (2011) *Family characteristics survey. Catalogue No. 4442.0* Canberra: Commonwealth of Australia.

Blustein J, Chan S & Guanais FC (2004) Elevated depressive symptoms among caregiving grandparents. *Health Services Research* **39** 1671–1689.

Brennan D, Cass B, Flaxman S, Hill T, Jenkins B, McHugh M, Purcal, C & Valentine K (2013) *Grandparents Raising Grandchildren: Towards recognition, respect and reward (SPRC Report 14/13)*. Sydney: Social Policy Research Centre, University of New South Wales.

Cowling V, Seeman MV & Göpfert M (2010) Grandparents parenting grandchildren when parents have a mental illness. *GEMS (Gateway to Evidence that MatterS)* **9**. Available at: http://www.copmi.net.au/images/pdf/Research/gems-edition-9-april-2010.pdf (accessed July 2017).

Cuddeback GS (2004) Kinship family foster care: a methodological and substantive synthesis of research. *Children and Youth Services Review* **26** 623–639.

Dunne EG & Kettler LJ (2008) Grandparents raising grandchildren in Australia: exploring psychological health and grandparents' experience of providing kinship care. *International Journal of Social Welfare* **17** 333–345.

Fitzpatrick M & Reeve P (2003) Grandparents raising grandchildren: a new class of disadvantaged Australians. *Family Matters* **66** (Spring/Summer) 54–57.

Fuller-Thomson E (2005) Canadian First Nations grandparents raising grandchildren: a portrait in resilience. *International Journal of Aging and Human Development* **60** 331–342.

Fuller-Thompson E & Minkler M. (2003) Housing issues and realities facing grandparent caregivers who are renters. *The Gerontologist* **43** 92–98.

Gerard JM, Landry-Meyer L & Roe JG (2006) Grandparents raising grandchildren: The role of social support in coping with caregiving challenges. *International Journal of Ageing and Human Development*, **62** 359–383.

Glaser K, Price D, Montserrat ER, de Gessa G & Tinker A (2013) *Grandparenting in Europe: Family policy and grandparents' role in providing childcare*. London: Grandparents Plus.

Grinstead LN, Leder S, Jensen S & Bond L (2003) Review of research on the health of caregiving grandparents. *Journal of Advanced Nursing* **44** 318–326.

Harriet (2008) Raising Sam: The experience of a grandmother raising her grandson from infancy. In: A Sved Williams & V Cowling (Eds) *Infants of Parents with Mental Illness: Developmental clinical cultural and personal perspectives* (pp 115–117). Brisbane: Australian Academic Press.

Hayslip B & Kaminski P L (2005) Grandparents raising their grandchildren: a review of the literature and suggestions for practice. *Gerontologist* **45** 262–269.

Hayslip B Jr, Shore R J & Emick MA (2006) Age health and custodial grandparenting. In: B Hayslip Jr & J Hicks Patrick (Eds) *Custodial Grandparenting: Individual cultural and ethnic diversity* (pp75–88). New York: Springer.

Horner B, Downie J, Hay D & Wichmann J (2007) Grandparent-headed families in Australia. *Family Matters* **76** 76–84.

House of Representatives Standing Committee on Family Community Housing and Youth (2009) *Who cares? Report on the inquiry into better support for carers*. Canberra: Commonwealth of Australia.

Hughes ME, Waite LJ, LaPierre TA & Luo Y (2007) All in the family: the impact of caring for grandchildren on grandparents' health. *The Journals of Gerontology Series B: Psychological Sciences and Social Sciences* **62** S108–119.

Jennifer (2008) '....No question'. In: A Sved Williams & V Cowling (Eds) *Infants of Parents with Mental Illness: Developmental clinical cultural and personal perspectives* (pp105–108). Brisbane: Australian Academic Press.

Jimenez J (2002) The history of grandmothers in the African-American community. *Social Service Review* **76** 523–551.

Kelley SJ, Whitley D, Sipe TA & Yorker BC (2000) Psychological distress in grandmother kinship care providers: the role of resources social support and physical health. *Child Abuse and Neglect* **24** 311–321.

Kohn SJ & Smith GC (2006) Social support among custodial grandparents within a diversity of contexts. In: B Hayslip Jr & J Hicks Patrick (Eds) *Custodial Grandparenting: Individual cultural and ethnic diversity* (pp199–223). New York: Springer.

Kolomer SR (2009) Grandparent caregivers' health and management of prescription medication. *Journal of Intergenerational Relations* **77** 243–258.

Kreider RM & Ellis R (2011) Living arrangements of children: 2009. *Current Population Reports* pp70–126. Washington, D.C.: U.S. Census Bureau.

Minkler M & Fuller-Thomson E (2005) African American grandparents raising grandchildren: a national study using the Census 2000 American Community Survey. *Journal of Gerontology: Series B Social Sciences:* **60B** S82–92.

Musil C, Warner C, Zauszniewski J, Wykle M & Standing T (2009) Grandmother caregiving family stress and strain and depressive symptoms. *Western Journal of Nursing Research* **31** 389–408.

Neely-Barnes SL, Graff JC & Washington G (2010) The health-related quality of life of custodial grandparents. *Health and Social Work* **35** 87–97.

Okagbue-Reaves J (2005) Kinship care: analysis of the health and well-being of grandfathers raising grandchildren using the grandparent assessment tool and the medical outcomes trust sf-36 health survey. *Journal of Family Social Work* **9** 47–66.

Sands RG & Goldberg-Glen R (2000) Factors associated with stress among grandparents raising their grandchildren. *Family Relations* **49** 97–105.

Sands RG, Goldberg-Glen R & Thornton PL (2005) Factors associated with the positive well-being of grandparents caring for their grandchildren. *Journal of Gerontological Social Work* **45** 65–82.

Sullivan R (2001) Fathering and children. *Family Matters* **58** 46–51.

Health related quality of life needs and preferences of children and adolescents who have parents with a severe mental illness

Judith Gellatly, Penny Bee, Lina Gega, Diane Hunter & Kathryn Abel

The prevalence of children and adolescents living with serious parental mental illness (CAPRI) remains unknown, although better care means this number is likely to be increasing (Abel *et al*, 2016). Current estimates indicate that up to 65% of adults with a serious mental illness (SMI) live with children under the age of 18 (Royal College of Psychiatrists, 2010; SCIE, 2011) and there is increasing concern about the lives of young people living with long term and serious mental illness.

While not all CAPRI will be adversely affected (Gladstone *et al*, 2011), it is now recognised that parental SMI is associated with a variety of short and long term adverse effects, in addition to the well-described risk of psychological and behavioural problems. CAPRI are also likely to experience poorer mental, physical, emotional and social health, as well as poorer well-being than children and adolescents of 'healthy' parents (e.g. Dean *et al*, 2010; van Santvoort *et al*, 2015; Siegenthaler *et al*, 2012). Furthermore, those who have a parent with an SMI are additionally likely to encounter more educational difficulties (SCIE, 2011). In adulthood, children have an increased risk of psychiatric morbidity, socio-occupational dysfunction, alcohol or substance misuse and premature death (Stanley, 2003). Consequently, the use of mental health services is also likely to be three times higher (Olfson *et al*, 2003). This means not only that they are an easily identifiable at-risk group, but also that preventative initiatives are important if these vulnerable young people are to fulfil their potential.

Despite children's well-being being considered vital, many practitioners working with families identify the challenges associated with addressing all needs within an organisation that has limited resources (Laletas *et al*, 2017). As the majority of children of parents with an SMI are unlikely to be, initially at least, experiencing any behavioural or mental health difficulties themselves, it is doubtful that they will receive any support, particularly if no issues of neglect or abuse have been identified. Moreover, evidence suggests that parents can be reluctant to seek support for their children because they fear being judged by others, often driven by stigmatising societal attitudes (Angermeyer & Matschinger, 2003). Currently, pathways of care and interventions for children of parents with mental illness are either non-existent or fragmented. Providing integrated care across adult and children's services and across health and social care services is difficult because of logistical and budgetary constraints.

Many children and adolescents may not identify themselves as having a 'need'. Understandably, they may fear the stigma of being involved with services, especially 'mental health services'. Many children see themselves as having an important role in their parent's well-being that may not be consistent with the perspectives of professionals who seek to reduce their burden of responsibility (Gladstone *et al*, 2011; Aldridge & Becker, 2003). Some may internalise their experiences and subsequent needs (Bayer *et al*, 2011). They may simply lack the ability to identify the effects that such life experiences are having because it is their 'normal'. As such, seeking help can be rare. Hinshaw (2005) referred to vulnerable children living in such circumstances as 'hidden children'.

The social and emotional well-being of children has been identified as a key priority in the UK in a number of publications including *Social and Emotional Wellbeing for Children and Young People* (NICE, 2013); *Think Child, Think Parent, Think family* (SCIE, 2011); *Working with Troubled Families* (Department for Communities and Local Government, 2012); and the *Children's and Young People's Strategy* (Department of Education, 2016). This is mirrored internationally in key policies such as *Children First: National guidance for the protection and welfare of children* in Ireland (Department of Children and Youth Affairs, 2011); *Children of Parents with a Mental Illness* (COPMI) *Framework for Mental Health Services 2010-2015* (NSW Department of Health, 2010); and the *Child Welfare Act* in Finland (Ministry of Social Affairs and Health, 2007). In these policies and publications, the responsibilities and roles that services should play are emphasised to ensure that children are safeguarded, and the vital importance of early intervention and integration of services is identified (e.g. Van Loon *et al*, 2015; Solantaus *et al*, 2010). There is also an underlying assumption that if a parent accesses services for a mental health problem, then the needs of their children will be addressed.

However, policy alone is often considered to be insufficient (Grant & Reupert, 2016) and some report that, despite guidelines, systematic responses are not apparent. To promote significant changes there is great need to develop clearly defined referral pathways and procedures, ensuring integration between services to enable children to access timely and appropriate support. Recent UK and European policy (*Social and emotional wellbeing for children and young people* (NICE, 2013); *Think Child, Think Parent, Think family* (SCIE, 2011); and *Child and Adolescent Mental Health in Europe: Infrastructures, policy and programmes* (Braddick *et al*, 2009)) is notable for highlighting the importance of health-related quality of life (HRQoL) beyond specific physical or mental health outcomes. It is widely agreed that HRQoL is a multi-dimensional, subjective concept where an individual's personal evaluation of their life is given weight alongside their physical and mental health status. Existing generic quality of life (QoL) models propose five core life domains:

1. Physical health.
2. Emotional health.
3. Social function.
4. Material well-being.
5. Environmental well-being.

(Bee *et al*, 2013)

It is questionable, however, whether these domains fully capture the experiences of children living with a parent with a mental illness (Crossroads Caring for Carers and The Princess Royal Trust for Carers, 2008).

In an attempt to explore gaps and disparities in generic HRQoL measurements and CAPRI experiences, Bee *et al* (2013) adopted a 'bottom-up' qualitative approach to develop a QoL model specific to children of parents with mental illness. This contrasted with existing service and research-driven approaches to HRQoL (Skevington *et al*, 1999) and was considered particularly important in giving a voice to this hidden group. Consultation via focus groups and individual interviews with key stakeholders (including young people and parents with lived experience of parental mental illness) endorsed five child-centred quality of life domains: emotional, social and economic well-being; family contexts and experiences; self-esteem; and self-actualisation. Similar findings have been documented via other consultation exercises and research (e.g. Gladstone *et al*, 2011; Royal College of Psychiatrists, 2010).

Despite the current interest and focus on HRQoL, to date it has been neglected as an outcome. A recent comprehensive systematic review sought to identify interventions that enhance HRQoL in children and adolescents with serous parental mental illness (Bee *et al*, 2014). The results were disappointing, if largely unsurprising: a number of studies focused on parents with mild to moderate depression, but only three considered parents with SMI. Furthermore, all were conducted over 20 years ago in the US, limiting the generalisability of their findings, and none of the interventions was child-centred or explored young people's HRQoL or emotional well-being, focusing solely on parental outcomes. It concluded that further work is urgently required to develop and evaluate child-centred interventions that aim to improve HRQoL in children and adolescents living with parents who have SMI.

A feasibility study is being led by The Centre for Women's Mental Health at The University of Manchester in collaboration with the NSPCC, Barnardo's, Northumberland Tyne and Wear NHS Foundation Trust and researchers and clinicians at the University of York, the Anna Freud Centre, London, University College London, University of Central Lancashire and Northumbria University (ISRCTN36865046). The aim is to develop and evaluate an intervention called 'Young SMILES', which will improve the HRQoL of CAPRI. It aims to build upon an existing NSPCC-developed intervention called 'Family SMILES' (Simplifying Mental Illness + Life Enhancement Skills), which underwent preliminary evaluation. This is a parent-centred intervention for families with an SMI in which in children aged 8-13 years had been identified as at risk of abuse or neglect. Its premise was to enhance parenting confidence and parental protective capacity and to improve the parent-child relationship.

A single-group, pre-post test evaluation of change on self-reported outcomes of strengths and difficulties, self-esteem and child abuse risk, highlighted a number of benefits for children, parents and families (Cass & Fernandes, 2014). These included:

1. For children, increased social functioning and confidence, reduced social isolation and reduced blame associated with parental illness.
2. For parents, less distress and unhappiness, a shift of thinking from own need to children's needs.
3. For families, a more relaxed atmosphere, openness about parental mental health, empathy between child and parent and shared responsibilities.

Additionally, the evaluation suggested that this intervention could be extended to reach a broader group of CAPRI, geographically and within the NHS.

The 'Young SMILES' project takes on the task of refining, delivering and evaluating this new child-centred, co-developed intervention to add to the scarce evidence base for this population and to explore the feasibility of engaging a potentially hard-to-reach group. Multiple potential approaches could be taken, but it is clear that specific systems need to be put in place to support these young people in a non-threatening and non-stigmatising manner. In the first phase of the study, we completed an extensive consultation exercise with children and adolescents alongside existing evidence and viewpoints from parents and practitioners to ensure the intervention would capture stakeholder priorities rather than service-centred priorities. This 'bottom-up' approach has been advocated for use in CAPRI by Bee *et al* (2013) as a viable way to identify gaps in current care. Using an inductive reasoning approach allows for open-ended and exploratory interactions with participants e.g. through focus groups or in-depth interviews. In Phase II of the project, 'Young SMILES' will pilot the feasibility and acceptability of a randomised controlled trial (RCT) to implement and evaluate a new manualised version of 'Young SMILES' compared with usual care.

One of the main challenges is that, currently, most children living with severe parental mental illness are 'nobody's business'. Unless these children have existing mental health or behavioural problems, or are 'at risk' of maltreatment from their parents, they do not receive any services. In our opinion, an important contribution of this project is its potential to deliver a targeted preventative initiative to optimise children's health and functioning through proactive interventions. Approaches such as 'Young SMILES' need to be integrated into care pathways somewhere along the health and social care service model and have significant implications for children's and adult services and how they integrate seamlessly, as well as for the commissioning of such 'in between' provisions by public and third sector services. This represents a new way of working across a more integrated system and is critical if we are to support children and adolescents living with parental mental illness and make their well-being 'everybody's business'.

References

Abel KM, Goldstein JM, Stanley N & Castle DJ (2016) Women and schizophrenia. In: Castle DJ and Abel KM (Eds) *Comprehensive Women's Mental Health*. Cambridge: Cambridge University press.

Aldridge J & Becker S (2003) *Children Caring for Parents with Mental Illness: Perspectives of young carers, parents and professionals*. Bristol: The Policy Press.

Angermeyer MC & Matschinger H (2003) The stigma of mental illness: effects of labelling on public attitudes towards people with mental disorder. *Acta Psychiatrica Scandinavica* **108** (4) 304–9.

Bayer JK, Rapee RM, Hiscock H, Ukoumunne OC, Mihalopoulos C & Wake M (2011) Translational research to prevent internalizing problems early in childhood. *Depression and Anxiety* **28** 50–7.

Bee P, Berzins K, Calam R, Pryjmachuk S & Abel KM (2013) Defining Quality of Life in the Children of Parents with Severe Mental Illness: A preliminary stakeholder-led model. *PLoS ONE* **8** (9) e73739.

Bee P, Bower P, Byford S, Churchill R, Calam R, Stallard P, Pryjmachuk S, Berzins K, Cary M, Wan M & Abel KM (2014) The clinical effectiveness, cost-effectiveness and acceptability of community-based interventions aimed at improving or maintaining quality of life in children of parents with serious mental illness: a systematic review. *Health Technology Assessment* **18** (8) 1–250.

Braddick F, Carral V, Jenkins R & Jané-Llopis E (2009) Child and Adolescent Mental Health in Europe: Infrastructures, policy and programmes. Luxembourg: European Communities.

Cass R & Fernandes P (2014) Evaluation of Family SMILES: Interim Report [online]. Available at: https://www.nspcc.org.uk/globalassets/documents/evaluation-of-services/family-smiles-interim-report.pdf (accessed July 2017).

Crossroads Caring and The Princess Royal Trust for Carers (2008) *At What Cost to Young Carers?*

Dean K, Stevens H, Mortensen PB, Murray RM, Walsh E & Pedersen CB (2010) Full spectrum of psychiatric outcomes among offspring with parental history of mental disorder. *Archives of General Psychiatry* **67** (8) 822–829.

Department for Communities and Local Government (2012) *Working with Troubled Families: A guide to the evidence and good practice*. London: DCLG.

Department of Children and Youth Affairs (2011) *Children first: National guidance for the protection and welfare of children*. Government Publications: Dublin.

Department of Education (2016) *Children and Young People's Strategy 2017-2027 Consultation Document*. Northern Ireland.

Department of Children and Youth Affairs (2011) *Children First: National guidance for the protection and welfare of children* [online]. Dublin: Department of Children and Youth Affairs. Available at: https://www.dcya.gov.ie/documents/Publications/ChildrenFirst.pdf (accessed July 2017).

Gladstone BM, Boudell KM, Seeman MV & McKeever PD (2011) Children's experiences of parental mental illness: a literature review. *Early Intervention in Psychiatry* **5** 271–289.

Grant A & Reupert A (2016) The impact of organisational factors and government policy on psychiatric nurses family focused practice with parents who have mental illness, their dependent children and families in Ireland. *Journal of Family Nursing* **22** (2) 199–223.

Hinshaw SP (2005) The stigmatization of mental illness in children and parents: developmental issues, family concerns, and research needs. *Journal of Child Psychology and Psychiatry* **46** 714–734.

Laletas S, Reupert A & Goodyear M (2017) "What do we do? This is not our area": child care providers' experiences when working with families and preschool children living with parental mental illness. *Children and Youth Services Review* **74** 71–79.

Ministry of Social Affairs and Health (2007) Finland Child Welfare Act (No. 417/2007; amendments up to 1292/2013).

NICE (2013) *Social and emotional well-being for children and young people*. NICE local government briefings.

NSW Department of Health (2010) *Children of Parents with a Mental Illness (COPMI) Framework for Mental Health Services 2010-2015*. NSWDoH.

Olfson M, Marcus SC, Druss B, Alan Pincus H & Weissman MM (2003) Parental depression, child mental health problems, and health care utilization. *Medical Care* **41** (6) 716–21.

Royal College of Psychiatrists (2010) *Parents as Patients: Supporting the needs of patients who are parents and their children* [online]. Available at: www.rcpsych.ac.uk/publications/collegereports/cr/cr164.aspx (accessed July 2017).

Siegenthaler E, Munder T & Egger M (2012) Effect of preventive interventions in mentally ill parents on the mental health of the offspring: systematic review and meta-analysis. *Journal of the American Academy of Child and Adolescent Psychiatry* **51** 8–17 e8.

Skevington SM (1999) Measuring quality of life in Britain: Introducing the WHOQOL-100. *Journal of Psychosomatic Research* **47** (5) 449–459.

Social Care Institute for Excellence (2011) Think child, think parent, think family: a guide to parental mental health and child welfare (SCIE Guide 30) [online]. Available at: http://www.scie.org.uk/publications/guides/guide30/index.asp (accessed May 2017).

Solantaus T, Paavonen EJ, Toikka S & Punamäki R-L (2010) Preventive interventions in families with parental depression: children's psychosocial symptoms and prosocial behavior. *European Child and Adolescent Psychiatry* **19** (12) 883–892.

Stanley N (2003) Working on the interface: identifying professional responses to families with mental health and child-care needs. *Health and Social Care in the Community* **11** 208–18.

Van Loon LMA, Van De Ven MOM, Van Doesum KTM, Hosman CMH & Witteman CLM (2015) Factors Promoting Mental Health of Adolescents Who Have a Parent with Mental Illness: A longitudinal study. *Child Youth Care Forum* **44** 777.

Van Santvoort F, Hosman CM, Janssens JM, van Doesum KT, Reupert A & van Loon LM (2015) The Impact of Various Parental Mental Disorders on Children's Diagnoses: A systematic review. *Clinical Child and Family Psychology Review* **18** (4) 281–99.

Working with multi-level relationships to improve child protection outcomes in families experiencing mental health difficulties

Nhlanganiso Nyathi and Jane Akister

This paper presents a systemic view of the relationships between families and professionals where there are child protection concerns. The interplay between parents and their children is affected by their mental well-being, their physical well-being, their temperament and their life circumstances. The interplay is bi-directional and there has therefore been an increasing imperative to use systemic approaches with families who are experiencing difficulties and who come to the attention of welfare services. Parent/child relationships are each bi-directional in that the child can affect the relationship as well as the parent: a depressed parent impacts on the child, but a fretful child impacts on the parent – the interactions are bi-directional and part of the multiple relationships that comprise the family system.

A systemic approach can be used to aid understanding of the family system and also to design appropriate interventions from the agencies and professionals involved (agencies as systems). The adoption of the systems approach is widely recommended in the social work context and practice. Munro (2011) in particular has repeatedly advocated the adoption of a systems approach to child protection practice. Among the benefits is that systems are trans-disciplinary (Laszlo & Krippner, 1998) and, according to Kirst-Ashman and Hull (2012), systems provide social workers with a conceptual perspective that emphasises interactions among the various components of child protection practices.

However, it is not always clear what influences the success or failure of a collaborative approach. While the systemic understanding of collaboration is proposed, there is still a lack of conceptual clarity about what constitutes successful collaboration and why it appears so difficult to achieve. Because collaboration includes children and young people, their parents or carers, and different professionals, it is important to explore their perspectives regarding which influences contribute to the success or failure of this approach. Given the social workers' lead role in particular, their perceptions and insights into this process are critical to

contributing not only to practitioners' knowledge, but also to effective collaboration (Nyathi & Akister, 2016).

SCIE (the Social Care Institute for Excellence) and Falkov have developed systemic approaches of particular interest here (SCIE, 2012; Falkov, 2012). SCIE's 'learning together' systems model has been used in a number of serious case reviews to identify issues that can help us learn from child deaths and improve practice.

The SCIE model uses learning from an individual case to provide a 'window on the system', looking into how well the local multi-agency safeguarding systems are operating. In serious case reviews, the SCIE systems model is commonly used to identify factors in the work environment that support good practice, and those that create unsafe conditions in which poor safeguarding practice is more likely to occur. Both the SCIE model and Falkov's Family Model can be used in conjunction with the Framework for the Assessment of Children in Need and Their Families tool (Department of Health, 2000), which was developed to provide a systematic way of assessing, analysing and identifying children and young people's needs within their families and within their wider context.

Falkov's Family Model is particularly relevant to the context of parental mental health, being specifically designed as an integrated approach that can help our understanding of the complex interplay between mental ill health in parents, the development and mental health of their children, and the relationships within family units that are affected by mental ill health (Falkov, 2012). According to this model, the mental health needs of an adult in the family affect the parenting and family relationships, thereby influencing the child's mental health and development. In turn, and importantly, the child's mental health and developmental needs affect the adult or parents, which in turn affects the parenting and family relationships. These bi-directional effects must be taken into account.

Falkov's Family Model builds on Crossing Bridges, a government sponsored 'train the trainers' programme with a family-focused approach that addresses the needs of children and their mentally ill parents (Mayes *et al*, 1998), and which has also been used to inform '*Think child, think parent, think family: a guide to parental mental health and child welfare*' (SCIE, 2009). Underpinning this guide was the recognition and promotion of the importance of a whole family focused approach. Central to this model is that it provides a framework for professionals to consider the parent, the child and the family as a whole system when assessing the needs of, and providing support for, families with a parent suffering from a mental health problem (Falkov, 2012).

Nyathi (2016) proposes combining components of the SCIE model and Falkov's Family Model to facilitate systemic analysis and understand how the multiple influences on interprofessional collaborative child protection are influenced by each other (see Figure 1 below). In the context of the external environment, Figure 1 highlights the interplay between the child, parent and family influences, the multi-level lead social worker and agency influences and the multi-level professionals and agency influences. Child protection outcomes are determined by the interplay between these influences and professional judgement and decision making, and hence by the level of participation each participant is able to engage with. The systemic

interactions between the interprofessional collaborators and their partnerships with and between family members suggests that some influences may either hinder or enable effective functioning of interprofessional collaborative child protection work because of the interconnectedness and interdependence of the system's various parts.

The importance of multi-level relationships in determining collaborative working is discussed later in this paper. Because social systems are open, the various influences from and on family members, lead social worker, various professionals and the external environment are synonymous with the systems inputs that influence the decision-making process and the output or outcomes for interprofessional collaborative child protection decision making and practice.

Considering children and young people's needs within their families and the wider environmental context there are three key domains: child development needs, parenting capacity and wider family and environmental factors. The systems approach has been criticised for failing to explain how structural issues such as power or poverty operate within society. Without this understanding, social workers are often criticised for not being

Figure 1: Conceptual framework for Interprofessional collaborative child protection decision making and practice which combines elements of SCIE learning together systems model and Falkov's systemic Family Model

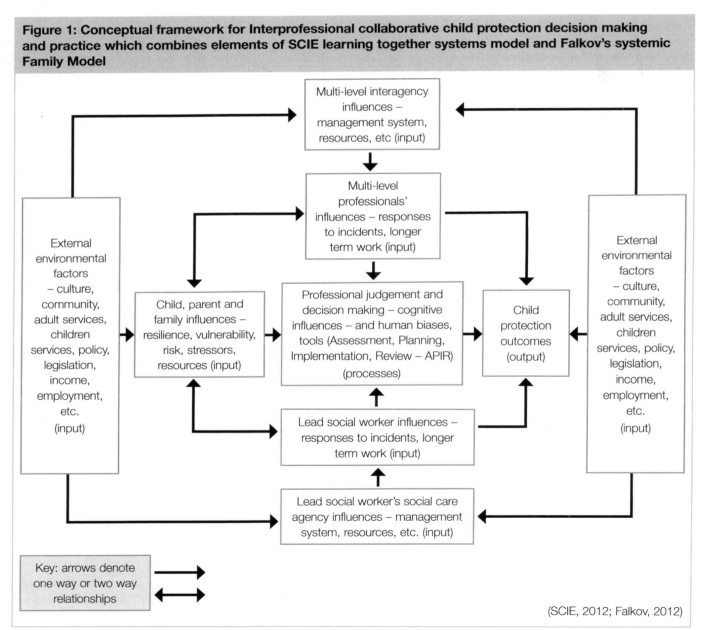

(SCIE, 2012; Falkov, 2012)

in a position to tackle the inequalities inherent therein. However, another strength of the conceptual framework proposed in Figure 1 is that it includes the identification of structural external environmental factors such as community, culture, policy, legislation and various services for the whole family, and it explores their interaction with other influences (Nyathi, 2016). Recognising the systemic interconnection and interactive relationships between the various influences, together with the social workers' knowledge and understanding of key influences, promotes the possibility of effective interprofessional collaborative child protection decision-making and practice.

While we are focusing here on parental mental health concerns, we also wish to note that mental ill health is not the only influence on parenting that may have an impact on the child's well-being. When parents become violent, abusive or substance dependent, their relationship with their children suffers and parenting may also deteriorate, leading to emotional instability or turbulence in the child. Similarly, physical illness in the parent or child can affect the parent/child relationship. This systemic conceptualisation could therefore be adopted in managing multiple parental problems often referred to as the toxic trio – substance use, mental health and domestic abuse – as well as with other common factors identified during child protection assessments (McGovern, 2012).

Clarity of professionals' roles

While there is increasing recognition that, theoretically, a systemic approach to families with child protection concerns is likely to be the most effective, this is not easy to implement, particularly where a number of different professionals are involved in assessing and intervening with the family. Thinking of 'agencies as systems' may begin to clarify positive approaches to working together. If professionals work in silos completing only their own tasks, collaboration fails.

According to Leutz (2005), integrated care comes in three varieties:

1. *Linkage*, in which health and social care providers attempt to work together more closely but still function within their respective silos, and with the constraints of anachronistic operating rules and separate funding streams.

2. *Co-ordination*, which involves the rebalancing of the system through purpose-built structures and mechanisms to bridge gaps between services and users, and also help to alleviate confusion, poor communication and the lack of information-sharing without overhauling the existing system.

3. *Full integration*, where responsibilities, resources and funding for long-term care from multiple sectors are combined under one roof, thus creating bundled financing, global management and unified service delivery.

Currently in the UK we operate with a mixture of 'linkage' and 'co-ordination', which means interprofessional relationships will need nurturing in respect of each family involved in child protection concerns. Combined with this, research indicates that professionals' relationships can also be stifled by the professionals' experiencing a lack of clear roles. Quite simply, professionals may know what is expected of them but be unclear how to achieve it. Social workers report that some of the barriers that impede the professionals' ability to play their roles effectively include:

→ Poor attendance at meetings.

→ Unavailability of reports, lack of action and non-engagement by professionals.

→ Lack of role clarity and responsibilities.

→ Competing professional and agency priorities.

(Nyathi, 2016)

Unsurprisingly, poor attendance at meetings can impede professionals' ability play their roles effectively and this can sometimes manifest itself in situations where, as well as not arriving at meetings and not sending in reports, professionals do not engage in meetings even when they do attend, which may also involve lack of engagement with any plans. For, example, quite often social workers are accused by other professionals for not taking action such as removing children into care before any work is done with the family, yet this illustrates a lack of understanding about each other's roles and responsibilities. For multi-level relationships to work professionals must assume and share responsibilities and expertise and not just defer everything to the lead social worker.

Multi-level relationship issues

While safeguarding children and young people is everyone's responsibility, it is important that all staff recognise their role in the safeguarding process and recognise and value the roles of others – relationship influences are interconnected in such a manner that they influence each other and they in turn are influenced by others, for example the influences of relationships with the lead social worker and family members will impact on each other. While there are advantages in bringing diverse professionals to work together there are also a number challenges. Where professionals do not trust each other they are not likely to have positive relationships. In child protection work there is rarely enough time for professionals and family members to build trust. Trust requires constant attention and nurturing in the tension-filled collaborative environments where professionals and their agencies may have different priorities.

Professionals' relationships can be antagonised by family members playing professionals off against each other. The tenuous relationships between family members and professionals can also be a source of tension and conflict between the professionals. Some of the barriers and conflicts that cause difficulties in professional relationships such as different agendas and real or perceived status differentials and values can have similar resonances in the relationships between professionals and family members. For example, Griffiths (2011) found that when adult mental health and social work professionals are in conflict, it seemed as if some professionals colluded with family members. Similarly, it has been found that GPs may withhold child protection information from other professionals because such information has been shared confidentially by the patient and medical ethics would therefore dictate that it should not be shared with other professionals. Part of the problem seems to rooted in concerns about antagonising relationships with family members. Family members' perception of professionals' use of power was the primary influence on shaping their views working collaboratively with professionals (Nyathi, 2016).

Inversely, family members can also negatively influence relationship with professionals. Where family members aggression and violence, relationships with professionals will be confounded (Neil, 2014). Relationships have been identified as pivotal to work with children and families and yet professionals have to work together and be prepared to 'think the unthinkable' and challenge these relationships to uncover evidence of dishonesty and skilful deceit by family members, as in Peter Connelly's injuries by the mother and her cohabitee (Laming, 2009). The bi-directional nature of relationships and the question of 'trust' underpins the role of supporting families with parental mental health in order to promote child well-being, but the professional, in a way, can never be trusted entirely by families since their role is to safeguard and protect the child's welfare. That welfare may be best served by the child remaining in the family, or it may be that the child is better served in an alternate environment.

In Nyathi's (2016) study, social workers identified a number of barriers and enablers to relationships that they perceived to be key to effective interprofessional child protection practice, including:

→ communication and information sharing between professionals

→ relationships between professionals

→ a clear and shared vision and goals by professionals

→ clarity of professionals' roles

→ professionals' relationships with family members

→ professionals' relationships with the lead social worker.

Social workers identified poor communication and lack of information sharing as one of the main causes of failure in relationships when professionals, family members and organisations are trying to work together to protect children and young people. The main barriers preventing good communication and information sharing included:

→ attitudinal barriers

→ lack of information and communication breakdowns

→ language barriers – professional jargon and diverse languages.

Attitudinal barriers include the attitude that 'somebody else will do that' and therefore no-one takes responsibility for a particular part of a plan. Sometimes the assumption is that someone else will notice. Participants felt that when professionals don't communicate it is difficult to work together as a team with common goals – the relationships just are not there. Social workers, on the other hand, perceived clear communication and information sharing as vital to the effectiveness of professionals' relationships.

...we have explored the complexity of working ...multi-level relationships. Families and professionals ...agenda – to promote the well-being of family ...the understanding of what is possible and of ...interests of different members is difficult ...different parts of the system may interpret ...differently. The relationships between ...family members, for example, the adult ...and the parent or the children's ...have to exist in the wider context of ...the professionals. None of these ...in the context of child protection

there is rarely enough time for trust between professionals and family members and between professional and professional to develop. The systems approach enables us to see where the relationship influences lie and this is a good starting point, but there will always be a need to recognise the barriers and enablers that determine the effectiveness of these relationships.

References

Department of Health (2000) *Framework for the Assessment of Children in Need and their Families* [online]. Available at: http://webarchive.nationalarchives.gov.uk/20130401151715/https:/www.education.gov.uk/publications/eOrderingDownload/Framework%20for%20the%20assessment%20of%20children%20in%20need%20and%20their%20families.pdf (accessed July 2017).

Falkov A (2012) *The Family Model Handbook: An integrated approach to supporting mentally ill parents and their children*. Hove: Pavilion Publishing & Media Ltd.

Griffiths J (2011) *Child Protection Versus Parental Mental Health Services* [online]. Available at: http://www.communitycare.co.uk/2011/04/01/child-protection-versus-parental-mental-health-services/ (accessed July 2017).

Kirst-Ashman K & Hull H (2012) *Generalist Practice with Organisations and Communities*. 5th ed. Belmont, USA: Brooks/Cole.

Laming L (2009) *The Protection of Children in England: A progress report* [online]. Available at: https://www.gov.uk/government/uploads/system/uploads/attachment_data/file/328117/The_Protection_of_Children_in_England.pdf (accessed July 2017).

Laszlo A & Krippner S (1998) Systems Theories: Their origins, foundations, and development. In: JS Jordan (Ed) *Systems Theories and A Priori Aspects of Perception* (pp47–74). Amsterdam: Elsevier.

Leutz W (2005) Reflections on integrating medical and social care: five laws revisited. *Journal of Integrated Care* **13** (5) 3–11.

Mayes K, Diggins M & Falkov A (1998) *Crossing Bridges: Training resources for working with mentally ill patients and their children*. Brighton: Pavilion Publishing.

McGovern W (2012) *Guide to the Toxic Trio: Managing multiple parental problems, substance use, mental health and domestic abuse* [online]. Available at: http://www.ccinform.co.uk/author/will-mcgovern/ (accessed May 2017).

Munro E (2011) *The Munro Review of Child Protection: Final report* [on-line]. Available at: https://www.gov.uk/government/uploads/system/uploads/attachment_data/file/175391/Munro-Review.pdf (accessed May 2017).

Neil R (2014) How Does Child Protection Work Affect Social Workers? *The Guardian* **23 July**. Available at: http://www.theguardian.com/social-care-network/2014/jul/23/child-protection-social-work-social-workers (accessed July 2017).

Nyathi N (2016) *Factors that are key influences to effective interprofessional collaborative child protection decision making and practice: social workers' perceptions*. Doctoral dissertation, Anglia Ruskin University.

Nyathi N & Akister J (2016) A Practitioner's perception of interprofessional collaboration influences in safeguarding children. *Childhood Remixed* (**6**).

SCIE (2009) Think Child, Think Parent, Think Family: A guide to mental health and chil welfare. London: SCIE.

SCIE (2012) *Learning together to safeguard children: a 'systems' model for case reviews* [online]. Available at: http://www.scie.org.uk/publications/ataglance/ataglance01.pdf (accessed July 2017).

Assessment, interventions and services

InterAct: A whole family approach to improving outcomes for children of parents with a mental illness

Mandy Bell, Jane Melton, Kate Moss and Rebecca Shute

The drive to establish whole family approaches in care services where a parent experiences mental ill health has, at best, been piecemeal. A thematic review of adult mental health and substance misuse services (Ofsted & CQC, 2013) indicated some concerning trends – that most services were not proactive in helping families to access early support, and that the majority of assessments did not provide a comprehensive and reflective analysis of the impact on the child of living with a parent with mental health difficulties. Furthermore, this study revealed that, in most cases when parents or carers had been admitted to hospital, joint working was poor and plans for discharge rarely took the children's needs into account. Children have indicated that they want to remain involved with their parents who have been admitted to a mental health hospital but that they require support from staff to manage the experience (O'Brien et al, 2011).

In this chapter we will be making the case for the introduction of a co-produced, family-oriented programme in mental health care. InterAct, developed and delivered through a partnership between Gloucestershire Young Carers, an independent charity, and 2gether NHS Foundation Trust, has consistently achieved positive outcomes for all family members and has the potential for making a sustained impact. In essence it embraces the principles embedded in 'The Family Model', the underpinning conceptual framework of *Crossing Bridges* (Falkov, 1998; 2012).

Why InterAct, a whole family approach?

The literature reveals a number of reasons why a whole family approach to mental health care may lead to more sustainable benefits to all family members. Parenting is a demanding role, and when adults also experience mental illness they may face additional challenges in carrying out that role. Furthermore, parents with mental illness and their children are more likely to face barriers to getting their health and social care needs addressed (ODPM, 2004). A substantial body of research, recognising the interplay of biological and environmental factors alongside parenting and family functioning, indicates that children whose parents

have a mental disorder have an increased risk of developing a mental disorder themselves (Meltzer et al, 2003; Parry-Langdon, 2008; Weissman et al, 2006; Cowling et al, 2004; Hosman et al, 2009).

Outcomes can be improved by increasing each family member's understanding of the parent's mental health problems (SCIE, 2012) and interventions such as 'Family Talk', developed by Beardslee et al (1997; 2003; 2007), have been shown to have sustained benefits over four years. This would suggest that a more inclusive, family-oriented approach to mental health care is desirable. Moreover, a review of individual, group and family-based interventions where a parent experiences a mental illness, including *Family Talk*, concluded that 'the risk of developing the same mental illness as the parent was decreased by 40%' (Siegenthaler et al, 2012).

> 'I overheard a conversation about my mum's mental health and because no one had explained it to me I thought that it was my fault, so I ran away from home.'

Gloucestershire young carer describing his experience.

> 'I know that it would help my child if we could talk together about my mental health issues but I just can't bring myself to have that first conversation.'

Comment from Gloucestershire parent.

InterAct, an overview

InterAct is a whole family programme for families where at least one parent experiences mental illness. Families are offered a sessional programme of intervention that supports and enables communication between family members in order to improve parent and child understanding of the mental illness and its impact on the whole family. The programme aims to identify family strengths and use them to develop strategies to minimise that impact and prevent children from taking on excessive or harmful caring roles. Before piloting the InterAct family programme, adult mental health services developed systems to raise the needs profile of these parents and children, promoting the distribution of co-produced whole-family information packs for parents and 'in-the-bag' information packs for their children.

InterAct was developed as a short-term intervention following a semi-structured pathway. It aims to improve every family member's understanding of the parent's mental illness; to open family communication; to support the development of individual and whole-family coping strategies; to reduce feelings of guilt, self-blame and fear; and to promote positive activity between parent and child. While having the flexibility to respond to emerging issues, it primarily addresses a range of factors that have the potential to both increase the resilience of children and to improve outcomes for both parent and child. InterAct supports and enables parents to overcome their fears about having that first conversation with their child about mental illness, in a manner appropriate to the needs of both parent and child, opening the door to more open communication beyond the duration of the programme. In identifying and addressing the impact of parental mental illness on all family members and by engaging family strengths in the development of individual and whole-family strategies, this short-term intervention has the potential to have a long-term impact.

The development of InterAct was informed by the voice of parents and children, supported by evidence from family programmes such as Family Talk (Beardslee *et al*, 1997; 2003; 2007) and an understanding of the impacts, risk and protective factors for parents and children (Falkov, 2012).

The InterAct service model

The implementation of InterAct was overseen by a steering group comprised of senior managers from Gloucestershire Young Carers and 2gether NHS Foundation Trust, two young carers and one parent. Young and adult experts by experience had an input in designing the InterAct leaflet, defining what terminology should be used, deciding where and how to deliver the programme, and helping to develop the post-programme stakeholder survey. Resources (Gloucestershire Young Carers, 2012; 2014) used during the programme had previously been developed by young carers.

Referral

The criteria for referral were minimal, requiring only that one parent was receiving a service from the NHS mental health trust; that at least one dependent child was between five and 17 years of age; and that the mental health care co-ordinator was committed to supporting the process. While initially developed to enable parents and children to access the service solely by referral from adult care co-ordinators, the programme quickly developed to broaden referral routes in order to improve access. During the one-year pilot phase, the majority of referrals did come directly from adult community mental health teams with an additional two referrals from schools and one self-referral. The requirement for engagement with the NHS mental health trust was also relaxed. This enabled one family to access the service despite the parent actively choosing not to engage with the allocated mental health worker, and another where the parent had recently been discharged to the care of their GP. In order to encompass prevention and early intervention alongside more embedded problems there was no requirement to define the impact of the parent's

mental health on the children. Nonetheless, referrers cited minor to substantial concerns for dependent children in each family referred to InterAct.

The programme

In response to the opinions of families, who report that engagement with a voluntary sector agency is likely to minimise feelings of anxiety, the programme is delivered primarily by Gloucestershire Young Carers. Mental health advice and some co-delivery of sessions were provided by the referring care co-ordinators or allocated mental health workers from 2gether NHS Foundation Trust. Referrers from the Trust were encouraged to attend the final session in order to ensure that the adult's care plan was revised appropriately and to help co-ordination with the child or children's support plans. Before engagement in the programme, bounds of confidentiality were routinely clarified and specific permission to share relevant information between the partners was agreed with families.

The initial concept of delivering a formulaic six to eight week programme was quickly adapted to enable the delivery of a semi-structured programme, responding to the specific and emerging needs of families. During the pilot phase this resulted in a variation of delivery from one to 14 sessions, with most being between seven and nine sessions.

Resources

The booklets *Minds, Myths and Me* (Gloucestershire Young Carers, 2014) and *Safe, Sorted and Supported* (Gloucestershire Young Carers, 2012) were used routinely, the former as a means of discussing mental illness in a child-friendly manner, and the latter as an aid to helping parents and children produce a plan for the child in case of a mental health or other crisis where the parent would not be available to the child.

Evaluation

Phase one of InterAct delivered direct support to 73 individuals made up of 35 parents and 38 children from 22 families. Six children under five years, one young adult and one parent who did not actively engage with the programme were deemed to be indirect beneficiaries as a consequence of being physically present during sessions and/or due to improvements in family relationships.

Parents and children were asked to complete a post-programme survey which had been co-developed by a range of stake holders including parents with mental health issues and their children. Questions were structured to determine both whether an outcome had been achieved and whether the outcome was as a result of InterAct. Where completion of the survey was problematic e.g. due to the age of younger children, the facilitator undertook interviews with the children or sought the views of parents.

On completion of the programme, home visits were arranged in order to evaluate the families' perspectives of outcomes. Surveys were completed by 11 parents and 12 children from nine families. Absence of funding beyond the one-year pilot phase necessitated a different approach to data collection, with surveys being posted to families rather than being completed on a home visit. This change in methodology significantly impacted on the acquisition of data as no postal surveys were returned.

Flowchart

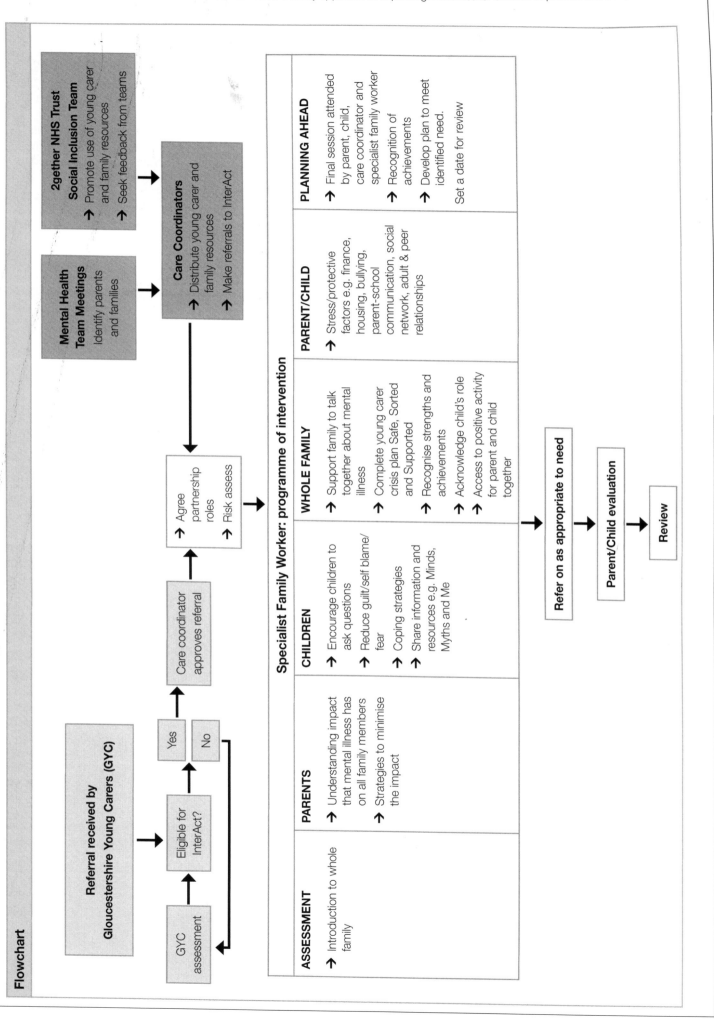

InterAct survey results

Young carer perspective of outcomes	
Improvement in understanding of parental mental ill health	100%
Improvement in mental health and well-being	82%
Improvement in indicators of emotional resilience	91%
Improvement in family relationships	82%

Parent perspective of outcomes	
Improvement in mental health and well-being*	100%
Improvement in ability to carry out parenting responsibilities when experiencing mental ill health	75%
Improvement in confidence and self-esteem	58%
Improvement in family relationships	67%

*most parents were receiving support from mental health services and as such it was not possible to delineate the impact of InterAct

Professional observation of family functioning and use of newly developed coping strategies supported the survey results.

Of the 22 families who have accessed InterAct, only two disengaged. In these instances, both expressed loss of trust in the service when advised of the intention to refer to local authority children's social care in response to emerging safeguarding concerns. A further five families continued to engage despite referrals to social care services, recognising that they needed a greater level of support. One family only needed one session to establish two-way communication between the parent and child about the parent's mental illness, which, in turn, resolved several issues. 151 of the 152 sessions proceeded as planned with only one 'no-show'. We would suggest that this high level of engagement was due to a combination of the value that the families found in the service and the ease of access, as visits were primarily undertaken in the family home or, for child-only sessions, in school.

Half of the families who engaged with InterAct reported recognising that they needed more quality time together and/or planned and undertook activities either as a family or between one parent and child. Two families realised that they could ask their wider family for additional on-going support, establishing sustainable coping strategies.

What people said about InterAct

In responding to the survey, several comments were made in free text areas by young people, their parents and health care workers, about the impact of their experience of the InterAct programme. Examples are provided in the boxes opposite, which illustrate how the programme and partnership approach was valued and had a positive impact.

Learning from InterAct – 9 key messages

1. **Take time to embed a new way of working with stakeholders**

   Where professional anxiety about the introduction of the InterAct programme existed there tended to be a belief that

Comments made by children and young people

'[InterAct] helped me to understand my mum's condition and how to help her through it.'

'My mum now understands how things affect me and my sister.'

'I now know what could happen to mum and what to do.'

'I know that M will look after me if mum is ill.'

Comments made by parents

'[InterAct] helped the children to find their voice.'

'[It's] not judgemental and doesn't take sides.'

'Just knowing she's there and that someone is interested in my family [is helpful].'

'Both myself and [my child] were in need of help whilst [dad] was away in hospital and you came and gave us a way through with your kindness and your genuine warmth, coupled with your experience and valuable knowledge.'

'[InterAct] enabled me to interact better with [my child].'

Comments made by care co-ordinators

'It opened a dialogue between the family and myself as care co-ordinator, which has been very helpful.'

'It was very helpful for the family as a whole to take on board that it is ok to talk about mum's mental health issues and how these are understood by a young person. It was also helpful for mum to receive a service that arose originally from concerns, in a very positive and supportive manner. It helped services to be able to feel assured that one of the risk issues identified [i.e. the impact of mum's mental health on the child] was being systematically and sensitively addressed. It also reduced the risk as it reduced the impact as the child was able to see that it wasn't her fault and develop a better insight.'

parents would not engage with the programme for fear of being judged as bad parents or the fear that their children would be removed from home for their own protection. For some, this suggested a potential risk to maintaining the level of trust required within a therapeutic relationship. A communication structure between agencies was built into the programme from the start. This was both integral to, and successful in, raising awareness of the service, building the momentum of referrals and building trusting relationships between agencies. After a slow start, InterAct was running at full capacity by the end of year one.

Care co-ordinators reported welcoming the service, which achieved above and beyond its objectives, in one case providing essential support for a very vulnerable family while the parent was on the waiting list for the eating disorder service. In another example, InterAct was observed by the care co-ordinator to address professional concerns relating to risk.

2. **Express the value of family work**

   The InterAct model has no requirement for sessions to be facilitated by a mental health clinician. In fact, families welcomed the fact that the facilitator's primary experience and skills were in family work, underpinned by a good mental health knowledge base and with access to advice and guidance from a mental health clinician if required. Crucial to this model of delivery is clarity and agreement by all stakeholders in relation to confidentiality and information sharing before each programme.

3. **Collaboration and interagency effort is key**

From the outset there was a clear expectation that the parent's care co-ordinator should attend the final InterAct session. In practice, where a care co-ordinator had been involved, they were present at 60% of the closing sessions. Logistical challenges included parent's being discharged from mental health services before completing InterAct; the requirement to travel to the family home rather than seeing the parent in clinic; difficulty in finding a mutually convenient time; or the need to respond to a crisis that coincided with the planned session. Where the care co-ordinator was unable to attend, some gave input in advance by telephone, some requested information to add to the parent's case notes, and all were sent a report of the session including reference to outcomes achieved and ongoing needs. One family did not want the child to meet the parent's mental health worker although they were happy for the child to know that there was someone supporting the parent. The programme worked to best effect where there was sound collaboration and team working across the participating organisations.

4. **Child and parent mental health is of equal importance**

Understanding parental and child mental health and the link between them is essential for a comprehensive approach. This needs to be supported by strong, informed and proactive leadership as well as integrated systems and processes across the adult-child service divide. Where a child is receiving a service from child and adolescent mental health services and their parent is receiving a service from adult mental health services, both care co-ordinators need to routinely be aware of this and need to communicate effectively in the best interests of both parent and child.

5. **Intensity of need varies**

The InterAct model proved to be effective across a wide spectrum of family compositions and circumstances. During phase one, the service was accessed by single parents and two-parent families; families from a variety of cultures; lone children and sibling groups; urban and rural; employed and unemployed parents; and both those with chronic and acute symptoms. While no discernible difference in outcomes was observed across the range of families, the level of concern was highest for lone parents with one child because these families face more stress factors and are able to call on fewer protective factors. Identifying ongoing support for these families was more challenging and completing *Safe, Sorted and Supported* (Gloucestershire Young Carers, 2012), a crisis plan for the child, was of greater importance.

6. **A flexible, family centred approach leads to positive outcomes**

Achieving positive outcomes was linked to flexibility. The initial concept of running a six- to eight-session programme was problematic for a number of reasons. Factors that required flexibility in relation to quantity of sessions included the number of children, the engagement of parents and family

priorities. At times issues such as housing and debt became the priority for some parents, which inevitably impacted on their ability to focus on discussions about their mental illness.

A flexible approach was also required in circumstances where the unwell parent could not engage. Where a father was being treated as an inpatient his permission was sought for the programme to be offered to the well parent and child, the father joining sessions when he was home. For another family, the father sat in an adjoining room with the connecting door open, over time building the confidence to attend a parent-child activity session run by Gloucestershire Young Carers and joining his family, his care co-ordinator, a representative from the child's school and the InterAct facilitator in the room for the final InterAct session.

7. **Engagement with schools helps to tackle stigma and increase access to services**

The benefits gained by involving schools was recognised to be of great importance, with 43% of children requiring no further support from the young carers service on completion of InterAct. Many parents had completely avoided or had struggled with discussing the additional challenges experienced by their children with the child's school, a sign of the stigma associated with mental illness. By building an understanding of the importance of communicating with schools and by being supported in making that first contact, parents were able to ensure that their child was provided with appropriate and sustainable support in relation to their education.

8. **It's all about timing**

Offering the service at a time that the family can invest in addressing the issues unsurprisingly proved to be important. Factors that created additional challenges included where families were engaged with multiple agencies or where a family member was commencing engagement with an additional support service.

9. **Speaking the same language helps**

Terminology and jargon are known to have the potential to exclude people. Of particular note within this service, labels such as 'young carer' and 'care co-ordinator' were misunderstood or problematic for some families. InterAct aimed to prevent children and young people taking on excessive or harmful caring roles. This preventative approach correlated to the identification and referral of families previously unknown to Gloucestershire Young Carers. In keeping with the majority of referrals to the organisation, most children and young people had not identified with the term 'young carer' before referral. While some children were identified as young carers over the course of the programme, many were not. In relation to the term 'care co-ordinator' most parents referred to 'my mental health worker' and children referred to 'my mum's/dad's support worker'. Reflecting the language used by the family and clarity about terminology was essential throughout.

Conclusion and recommendations for the future

There can be no better validation of InterAct than that provided by the families who have engaged with it. The 99.3%

attendance rate is a strong indicator of the value that young people and their parents put on the InterAct service. This, supported by the outcomes achieved by families, suggests that InterAct can and has made a real difference to many of the individuals and families who engaged with the service. In the words of one young person:

'It's been life changing.'

From an organisational perspective, we would highlight that this partnership between a small third-sector organisation, an NHS mental health trust, and young and adult experts by experience, provided substantial scope for flexibility in design, bringing together a wealth of information, skills, networks, resources, expertise and passion to drive important developments.

On reflection, we have a number of recommendations for the further development of the InterAct model.

Recommendation 1: recognise the need for ongoing support

Individuals and families were able to develop positive coping strategies over the course of the programme. However, it cannot be presumed that these strategies will continue to be embedded routinely. As such we would recommend a limited period of occasional one-to-one follow up, particularly for the children and young people. This could potentially be with a mentor, befriender or youth worker.

Recommendation 2: encourage engagement in complimentary programmes

A number of parents recognised that they had lost the motivation to organise and undertake positive activities with their children. This impacted on the connection between parent and child and the social integration of families within their communities. For some families, engagement with InterAct was sufficient to 're-ignite' this behaviour, but for others this presented a real challenge. It would be of benefit to any family that remained socially isolated to have access to further support specifically addressing this issue. There are undoubtedly a range of mechanisms to achieve this outcome – Gloucestershire Young Carers, for example, runs child and parent sessions which reintroduce parents and their children to positive, fun and healthy activities, promoting positive parenting, the parent-child relationship and connection between families. Given the positive impact of community engagement, an emphasis on further supporting the family to this end would offer the potential to establish more sustainable social inclusion.

While increased support from schools and improved parenting and family relationships meets the needs of many children, some require further support. One issue that frequently arises for children of parents with a mental illness is a feeling of being isolated, or of being the only person in their situation. For these children we would recommend access to a group programme such as Gloucestershire Young Carers' 'Us Too' support group (Wright & Bell, 2001) for children living with a family member who experiences mental ill health.

Recommendation 3: InterAct with and beyond statutory services

The involvement of adult mental health care co-ordinators has been wholly positive, although this does preclude families from accessing the service where the parent is below the threshold for statutory mental health services. Recognising the intermittent nature of some mental health disorders and the benefits of prevention and early intervention, we would recommend that InterAct is accessible to all families where a parent experiences mental illness and where the symptoms of that illness impact on parenting and children. Where the parent is accessing statutory mental health services the involvement of the care co-ordinator is invaluable.

InterAct aims to empower families to develop strategies that can reduce their reliance on services. The success of this service model, at least in the short term, is demonstrated by the increased awareness of the issues by, and improved support from, schools, and the number of parents who are able to meet their children's needs on completion of the programme, requiring no ongoing support from children's services.

Acknowledgements

The authors of this chapter would like to recognise the significant contribution of our colleagues Lucy Garden and Alison Curson, who were both pivotal in establishing the project. We would also like to express our gratitude to the parent and two young people who gave up so much of their time to help steer the project throughout its development. Phase one of InterAct was funded by Carers Trust with funding from the Department for Education as part of the Integrated Interventions for England award.

References

Beardslee WR, Wright EJ, Salt P, DRezner K, Gladstone T, Versage EM & Rothberg PC (1997) Examination of children's responses to two preventive intervention strategies over time. *Journal of the American Academy of Child & Adolescent Psychiatry* **36** (2) 196–204.

Beardslee WR, Gladstone TRG, Wright EJ & Cooper AB (2003) A family-based approach to the prevention of depressive symptoms in children at risk: evidence of parental and child change. *Paediatrics* **112** (2) e119–131.

Beardslee WR, Wright EJ, Gladstone TRG & Forbes P (2007) Long-term effects from a randomized trial of two public health preventive interventions for parental depression. *Journal of Family Psychology* **21** (4) 703–713.

Cowling V, Luk ESL, Mileshkin C & Birleson P (2004) Children of adults with severe mental illness: mental health, help seeking and service use. *The Psychiatrist* **28** 43–46.

Falkov A (Ed) (1998) *Crossing Bridges: Training resources for working with mentally ill parents and their children – An evidence based reader.* Brighton: Pavilion Publishing & Department of Health.

Falkov A (2012) *The Family Model Handbook: An integrated approach to supporting mentally ill parents and their children.* Hove: Pavilion Publishing and Media Ltd.

Gloucestershire Young Carers (2012) *Safe, Sorted and Supported: A guide to help young people plan ahead* [online]. Available at: https://www.flipgorilla.com/p/24942796347540972/show (accessed July 2017).

Gloucestershire Young Carers (2014) *Minds, Myths and Me: A fact pack for young people who live with someone with a mental illness* [online]. Available at: https://www.flipgorilla.com/p/24919606124610322/show (accessed July 2017).

Hosman C, van Doesum K & van Santvoort F (2009) Prevention of emotional problems and psychiatric risks in children of parents with a mental illness in the Netherlands: I. The scientific basis to a comprehensive approach. *Australian e-Journal for the Advancement of Mental Health* **8** (3).

Meltzer H, Gatward R, Corbin T, Goodman R & Ford T (2003) *Persistence, Onset, Risk Factors and Outcomes of Childhood Mental Disorders* [online]. Office for National Statistics. Available at: https://www.ons.gov.uk/ons/rel/psychiatric-morbidity/persistence--onset--risk-factors-and-outcomes-of-childhood-mental-disorders/2002-survey/childhood-mental-disorders.pdf (accessed July 2017).

O'Brien L, Anand M, Brady P & Gillies D (2011) Children visiting parents in inpatient psychiatric facilities: perspectives of parents, carers, and children. *International Journal of Mental Health Nursing* **20** (2) 137–43.

Office of the Deputy Prime Minister (2004) *Mental Health and Social Exclusion, Social Exclusion Unit Report*. London: ODPM.

Ofsted & Care Quality Commission (2013) *What about the children: Joint working between adult & children's services: What about the children?* [online]. Available at: www.ofsted.gov.uk/resources/130066 (accessed June 2017).

Parry-Langdon N (Ed) (2008) *Three years on: Survey of the development and well-being of children and young people*. Newport: Office for National Statistics.

Social Care Institute of Excellence (2012) *At a glance 09: Think child, think parent, think family* [online]. Available at: http://www.scie.org.uk/publications/ataglance/ataglance09.asp (accessed July 2017). London: SCIE.

Siegenthaler E, Munder T & Egger M (2012) Effect of preventive interventions in mentally ill parents on the mental health of the offspring: systematic review and meta-analysis. *Journal of the American Academy of Child & Adolescent Psychiatry* **51** (1) 8–17.

Weissman MM, Wickramaratne P, Nomura Y, Warner V, Pilowski D & Verdeli H (2006) Offspring of depressed parents: 20 years later. *American Journal of Psychiatry* **163** (6) 1001–1008.

Wright S & Bell M (2001) The 'Us Too' group: a psychodynamic perspective on the impact of parental mental ill-health. *Young Minds Magazine* **(50)** 16-20.

Pharmacological treatment of mental illness and the role of the family

Eleni Palazidou

Introduction

One in every five people worldwide has suffered with a mental disorder in the last year and 30% of us will experience a mental illness in our lifetime. The World Health Organisation (WHO) reported an 18% increase in the prevalence of depression between 2005 to 2015, which is already the leading cause of ill health and disability worldwide.

Effective drug treatments, together with community care service provision, has normalised people's lives and enabled those with severe and enduring mental illness to have family lives and be parents (Nimganonkar et al, 1997). In the UK at any given time about 10% of women and 5% of men with a mental disorder will be parents. The percentage of women with a psychotic illness who were mothers in 2001 was as high as 63% (Howard et al, 2001) and this figure may be rising. Ten to 15% of children in the UK live with a parent who has a mental disorder and 28% of these are the children of a lone parent with a mental disorder (Royal College of Psychiatrists, 2011).

The benefits of being part of a family unit may be offset by the stress of the responsibilities that this entails as parents with mental illness have to cope with the dual demands of ill health and parenting. Mental disorders affect not only the patient's own life but also the well-being of their families, and in particular their children.

Parental mental illness can affect children in a number of ways. They may develop the same mental disorder as the parent and also experience other psychological problems, which can either be 'internalising' (negative emotions, depressive symptoms and anxiety) or 'externalising' (hyperactivity, aggressiveness and other behavioural problems) (Siegenthalen et al, 2003). It is very encouraging, however, that appropriate treatment interventions have been shown to decrease the risk of such psychological problems in children by as much as 40% (Siegenthalen et al, 2003).

Box 1: Treatment objectives

→ Best possible health and quality of life outcomes in the short and long term.

→ Achieve and maintain maximum symptom control.

→ Return to premorbid functional state.

→ Prevention of any deterioration.

→ Minimise adverse effects of medication.

Exploring the difficulties facing parents with mental illness, one qualitative study identified problems with medication as one of the main themes (Ackerson, 2003). However, with appropriate support and the positive involvement of the family this can be managed to the benefit of all concerned.

Drug treatment issues

Drugs are essential to the treatment of severe and enduring mental illness, and in most cases they need to be taken long term. With the variety of drugs available it is possible, with the patient's co-operation, to keep the illness at bay and enable people to have a good quality of personal and family life.

Effectiveness of treatment

It is essential that pharmacological treatments and other interventions should aim, as much as possible, to achieve full symptom control and not just an improvement (see Box 1 for treatment objectives). The presence of residual symptoms is associated with impaired functioning (Altshuler et al, 2001) and an increased likelihood of relapse of the illness. One common reason for poor treatment effectiveness is lack of compliance with the medication.

Compliance/adherence

Despite their effectiveness in alleviating the symptoms of mental conditions, adherence to psychotropic medications is far from ideal. Patients with severe mental health problems are less likely to take their medication as prescribed and half of those with the diagnosis of schizophrenia fail to do so. Compliance issues are not limited to psychosis and it is known that premature discontinuation of antidepressant medication is a problem in people with depression.

There are various reasons for people failing to take their medication as prescribed, such as lack of insight, fear of being labelled and experiencing side effects, among others.

People often stop their medication once they feel well without realising that symptom control doesn't always mean cure of the condition. In many cases the medication should be continued for a variable period of time after achieving remission (depending on the nature of the illness) to minimise the risk of relapse, and sometimes it needs to stay for the long term to ensure remission is maintained. Severe enduring mental illness behaves like any chronic physical illness, such as diabetes or epilepsy for example, where the pharmacological treatment cannot eradicate the cause of the condition but it can effectively control the symptoms.

Adverse effects

Unfortunately, drugs sometimes have undesirable effects, which is one of the main reasons why people stop taking them. Undesirable drug effects may occur with many medications for a number of reasons, including the inherent pharmacological properties of the drug, interactions with other psychotropic drugs, drugs given for the treatment of non-psychiatric conditions or drugs bought over the counter (including various herbal medicines), and even some foodstuffs. Abrupt discontinuation of a drug after regular use for a period of time can also cause adverse reactions.

Drugs currently used for the treatment of mental disorders are generally associated with less serious side effects and are better tolerated than the older generation of psychotropic drugs. There is also a wider range of drugs available, which enables the prescriber to tailor a pharmacological treatment to the individual person and their needs, not just the diagnosis. Nevertheless, psychotropic drug treatment is not uncommonly associated with side effects, and their presence may lead to non-compliance resulting in a relapse of the illness.

The adverse effects that patients most commonly complain of in relation to psychotropic drugs are weight gain and sleep problems, mainly sedation (McIntyre, 2009). These symptoms, together with movement disorders (stiffness, tremors and physical restlessness, for example) are considered by patients to have the most negative effect on their quality of life (Angermeyer & Matschinger, 2000), and these are the ones that are most commonly associated with stopping or changing medication (Galinska-Skok et al, 2010).

It should also be noted that some medications, such as lithium, clozapine and some others, need regular monitoring,

---

Box 2: Therapeutic alliance and concordance

→ Adequate information about the nature of the illness and the need for treatment and its possible duration.

→ A positive message about the treatability (when appropriate).

→ Explain that drugs are not addictive (where appropriate), and that they do not alter one's personality nor affect intelligence.

→ Inform patient about potential for dependence with some medications i.e. benzodiazepines.

→ It may take some time before the symptoms start showing significant improvement.

→ They may experience some side effects – inform on common and serious side effects and what to do if these occur.

→ Medication could be changed if it does not work or they find any side effects unacceptable.

→ Regular reviews of the patient's mental and physical state and any risks (related to illness or medication) offers further reassurance and support, helps ensure compliance and allows prompt interventions as appropriate

Involve the family!

---

with blood tests done at different time intervals. This may be a further burden to the patient.

Physical health in the mentally ill

The World Health Organisation (WHO) has sent a global warning that people with severe mental disorders (schizophrenia, bipolar disorder, moderate to severe depression) have a shorter life span, dying 10–25 years earlier than the general population. A large percentage of this premature mortality is accounted for by physical health problems (Baandrup et al, 2010; Osby et al, 2001), with cardiovascular disease (coronary heart disease, atherosclerosis, hypertension and stroke) being one of the leading causes. Type 2 diabetes, respiratory diseases and infections such as HIV, hepatitis and tuberculosis are also prevalent.

These medical conditions are associated with preventable risk factors, such as smoking, physical inactivity, obesity and the side effects of psychiatric medication. The socio-economic consequences of severe mental disorders, such as increased risk of poverty, unemployment, social isolation and social stigma, which increase psychological stress and unhealthy behaviours (such as smoking and unhealthy eating etc.) contribute to the physical and mental health problems faced by people with mental illness.

The sad reality is that people with mental illness do not receive the same standard of physical health care as the general population, worldwide, and the WHO stresses the need for increasing access to quality care for patients with severe mental disorders and to improve the diagnosis and treatment of coexisting physical conditions. NICE guidelines (UK) give more specific guidance on monitoring weight, blood pressure, lipid profile and blood sugar levels with further advice on encouraging and educating patients, as appropriate, to maintain a healthy diet and exercise regularly in order to prevent cardiovascular diseases and diabetes.

A very important, and possibly more neglected, reason that people with a mental illness are at higher risk of serious physical conditions is that they are less likely to seek help for their ill health or to effectively manage early signs of illness.

The role of the family

The primary factor in motivating people with a mental illness to engage in treatment is the desire to maintain the parenting role (Mowbray et al, 2001). The General Medical Council (GMC) recommends that patients and doctors make decisions together about treatment or care. It also suggests that, for the relationship between doctor and patient to be effective, it should be a partnership based on openness, trust and good communication. This could and should be extended to include the family of the patient, ensuring at the same time that the patient's wishes and confidentiality are respected. The family can play an invaluable role in supporting the patient to take care of both their mental health, with adherence to the necessary medication and other treatments, as well as their physical health.

There is ample evidence that involving families is highly beneficial and can improve outcomes from pharmacological treatments (Glick et al, 2011). One study (integrating eight systematic reviews), which aimed to develop practice guidelines for social workers working with adults who do not adhere to prescribed psychiatric medications, identified several themes that were associated with better adherence. These included collaboration between patients and providers regarding medication decisions, consistent follow-up care and a comprehensive network of professionals and caregivers who support clients in their use of medication (Townsend, 2009). Psychoeducation of the patient and family improves adherence with medication, reduces relapses with fewer hospitalisations and, in some cases, also improves the person's social and global functioning and their overall quality of life. Multi-family psychoeducation groups are associated with significantly improved problem-solving abilities and a reduced burden on families (McFarlane *et al*, 2003). However, in order to be effective in improving adherence with medication, psychoeducation requires a concrete problem-solving or motivational approach (such as reminders, self-monitoring tools, cues and reinforcements) rather than more broadly based treatment interventions, as well as reinforcement techniques and consolidation of the gains (Zygmunt *et al*, 2002).

For optimum results, psychoeducation needs to tackle a number of issues in addition to diagnosis and medication, such as learning how to reduce stress in the family environment, a well-known factor in causing relapse of illness (Falloon *et al*, 1982) and providing advice on healthy living. Brief family interventions such as education, which increase self-efficacy regarding coping, expand knowledge about the illness and reduce distress among family members, can be effective (Drapalski *et al*, 2009). Family interventions have a positive effect on the burden of relatives of people with a mental illness including psychological distress, and a positive effect on the relationship between patient and relative and family functioning (Cuipers, 1999).

Working together

Implementing family involvement carries additional challenges, as it requires a cultural and organisational shift towards working with families (Eassom *et al*, 2014). Family psychoeducation efforts that have been successful are those based on consensus at all levels, including patients and their family members, and have provided ample training, support and supervision. Very importantly they have also maintained a long-term perspective (Dixon *et al*, 2001). A proper integration of health and social services can go a long way towards achieving better outcomes for people with a mental illness and their families. It will facilitate and improve on the Care Programme Approach (CPA), which aims to bring together relevant professionals and the patient and his/her carer in order to agree on a comprehensive and achievable care plan both in the short and long-term. At present, the onus is on the health services alone to ensure this. The co-operation and collaboration between all relevant stakeholders, including the health and social services professionals with the patient and his/her family, are essential to the success of the care plan.

Important issues relevant to drug treatment – misconceptions and fear

Patients and their families cannot work effectively with professionals if they are not well informed and supported. Unfortunately, there are a lot of hurdles to overcome in order

---

Box 3: Involving the family

→ Family therapy as necessary to minimise stressful conditions.

→ Information on the diagnosis and nature of the condition (i.e. factors that influence its presentation and course).

→ Clear information on medication matters:

  → What the prescribed drugs are expected to do.

  → What the possible common and serious side effects are.

  → How and when the medication should be taken and for how long.

  → What to do if worried about troublesome side effects or lack of compliance and who to contact (nominated person with telephone/email).

→ Information on the high risk of physical health problems:

  → The importance of encouraging a healthy lifestyle (healthy diet and exercise, stop smoking etc.)

  → Dealing promptly and effectively with any emerging physical health problems and encouraging yearly or more frequent checks by GP as appropriate.

→ Regular meetings with the family for support and encouragement and advice on dealing with any difficulties.

---

to achieve optimum results in the treatment of people with a mental illness compared to those with physical ill-health, the main ones being the stigma of mental illness and the misconceptions around medication. These difficulties can be overcome to a great extent when professionals and patients/families work in alliance. It is essential to overcome the stigma, demystifying the nature of mental illness and the way medications work; this goes a long way towards building patient and family confidence in the treatability of the mental condition and the possibility of a much improved quality of life.

An assessment of the family environment by a professional such as a social worker or other can identify any factors in the functioning of the family that need to be dealt with in order to enhance the patient's chances of getting better and staying well. This might include any use of alcohol or illicit drugs, and conditions and behaviours that are associated with stress for the patient such as threatening or violent behaviour, or 'expressed emotion', all of which are likely to encourage relapse of illness. As far as drug treatment is concerned, the patient and the family needs to have adequate information so that they can make an informed decision not only when consenting but also in order to stay the course. The key pieces of information needed are:

1. What is the nature of the condition that needs to be treated and how is the medication expected to influence this?

2. What are the common and serious possible side effects of the medication?

3. What to do in the event of any problems or worries about medication (see Box 3).

4. The importance of taking good care of physical health.

Very importantly, children also need to be given relevant information about their parent's illness and the effects of treatment, as appropriate for their age.

Conclusion

Mental disorders are generally treatable conditions and, with close co-operation between professionals and patients/families, we can achieve optimum outcomes for people with a mental illness with good control of the illness and better quality of life.

References

Ackerson BJ (2003) Coping with the dual demands of severe mental illness and parenting: the parents' perspective. *Families in Society* **84** (1) 109–118.

Angermeyer MC & Matcshinger H (2000) Neuroleptic treatment and quality of life: a patient survey. *Psychiatrische Praxis* **27** (2) 64–68.

Baandrup L, Gasse C, Jenhsen VD, Glenthoi BY, Nordentoft M, Lublin H, Fink-Jensen A, Lindhardt A & Mortensen PB (2010) Antipsychotic polypharmacy and risk of death from natural causes in patients with schizophrenia: a population-based nested case-control study. *Journal of Clinical Psychiatry* **71** (2) 103–108.

Cuijpers P (1999) The effects of family interventions on relatives' burden: a meta-analysis. *Journal of Mental Health* **8** 275–285.

De Hert M, Correll CU, Bobes J, Cetkovich-Bakmas M, Cohen D, Asai I, Detraux J, Gautam S, Möller HJ, Ndetei DM, Newcomer JW, Uwakwe R & Leucht S (2011) Physical illness in patients with severe mental disorders. I. Prevalence, impact of medications and disparities in health care. *World Psychiatry* **10** (1) 52–77.

Dixon L, McFarlane WR, Lefley H, Lucksted A, Cohen M, Falloon I, Mueser K, Miklowitz D, Solomon P & Sondheimer D (2001) Evidence-based practices for services to families of people with psychiatric disabilities. *Psychiatric Services* **52** (7) 903–910.

Drapalski AL, Leith J & Dixon L (2009) Involving families in the care of persons with schizophrenia and other serious mental illnesses: history, evidence, and recommendations. *Clinical Schizophrenia and Related Psychoses* **3** (1) 39–49.

Eassom E, Giacco D, Dirik A & Priebe S (2014) Implementing family involvement in the treatment of patients with psychosis: a systematic review of facilitating and hindering factors. *BMJ Open* **4**:e006108. doi: 10.1136/bmjopen-2014-006108.

Falloon IRH, Boyd JL, McGill CW, Razani J, Moss HB & Gilderman AM (1982) Family management in the prevention of exacerbations of schizophrenia: a controlled study. *The New England Journal of Medicine* **306** 1437–1440.

Galinska-Skok B, Paterakis P, Bubrovszky M, Thomas P, Perdriset G & Pani L (2010) Reasons for switching between antipsychotic drug treatments – the international antipsychotic drug substitution registry. *Eur Neuropsychopharmacology* **20** (suppl 3) P.3.c.053.

Glick ID, Stekoll AH & Hays S (2011) The role of the family and improvement in treatment maintenance, adherence, and outcome for schizophrenia. *Journal of Clinical Psychopharmacology* **31** (1) 82–5.

Howard LM, Kumar R & Thornicroft G (2001) Psychosocial characteristics and needs of mothers with psychotic disorders. *British Journal of Psychiatry* **178** (5) 427–432.

McFarlane WR, Dixon L, Lukens E & Lucksted A (2003) Family psychoeducation and schizophrenia: a review of the literature. *Journal of Marital and Family Therapy* **29** (2) 223–245.

McIntyre RS (2009) Understanding needs, interactions, treatment, and expectations among individuals affected by bipolar disorder or schizophrenia: the UNITE global survey. *Journal of Clinical Psychiatry* **70** Suppl 3:5-11.

Mowbray CT, Oyserman D, Bybee D, MacFarlane P & Rueda-Riedle A (2001) Life circumstances of mothers with serious mental illnesses. *Psychiatric Rehabilitation Journal* **25** (2) 114–123.

Nimgaonkar VL, Ward SE, Agarde H, Weston N & Ganguli R (1997) Fertility in schizophrenia: results from a contemporary US cohort. *Acta Paediatrica Scandinavica* **95** (5) 364–369.

Osby U1, Brandt L, Correia N, Ekbom A & Sparén P (2001) Excess mortality in bipolar and unipolar disorder in Sweden. *Archive of General Psychiatry* **58** (9) 844–50.v

Royal College of Psychiatrists (2011) CR164: *Parents as patients: supporting the needs of patients who are parents and their children* [online] Available at: http://www.rcpsych.ac.uk/files/pdfversion/CR164.pdf (accessed July 2017).

Siegenthaler E, Munder T & Egger M (2012) Effect of preventive interventions in mentally ill parents on the mental health of the offspring: systematic review and meta-analysis. *Journal of the American Academy of Child & Adolescent Psychiatry* **51** (1) 8–17.

Townsend L (2009) How effective are interventions to enhance adherence to psychiatric medications? Practice implications for social workers working with adults diagnosed with severe mental illness. *Journal of Human Behavior in the Social Environment* **19** (5) 512–530.

Zygmunt A, Olfsen M, Bover CA & Mechanic D (2002) Interventions to improve medication adherence in schizophrenia. *American Journal of Psychiatry* **159** (10) 1653–64.

C-Change: An approach to assessing parental capacity to change

Dendy Platt, Katie Riches and Wendy Weal

C-Change is a flexible approach to assessing parents' capacities to change, where their children are in need or at risk of maltreatment. It combines two essential elements – understanding and action. The first involves assessing and understanding barriers and facilitators affecting the parents' attempts to change their behaviour. The second involves time-limited assessment of the parents' actions as they try to make changes (with appropriate support and intervention).

It was developed by Dendy Platt and Katie Riches at the University of Bristol for use primarily by social workers in children and families settings, but the principles behind its use are suitable for use in other professional areas. In this chapter, we begin by setting out the potential benefits of C-Change and then we explore the basis of the approach and the key aspects that are involved in using it. We finish by outlining the results of an evaluation.

The C-Change approach is intended to support:

→ Clear thinking and professional judgement.

→ Better decision-making for children, including reduced delays and greater coherence between assessments and decisions.

→ Improvements in the quality and accuracy of assessments. The addition of parental capacity to change into the analysis or formulation of an assessment enables the social worker to follow a more logical analytical process.

→ Increased involvement of parents in developing meaningful, manageable and measurable goals for change. This enhances the chances of parents working with the plans for their children and avoids parents feeling they have been set up to fail.

→ Improved outcomes for children, arising from improvements in decisions themselves and improved speed of decisions. The potential here is to identify and address barriers and facilitators to change enabling practitioners to offer the right help or intervention to parents at an earlier stage. Thus improving the chances that their children's needs can be addressed within their developmental timescales.

→ Greater cost-effectiveness, achieved largely through a reduction in repeat assessments

→ Greater accuracy in decision-making.

→ Greater credibility of court reports and a consequent reduction in the need for expert witnesses.

Theory/research

It is important to note at the outset that parental capacity to change is different from parenting capacity. Parenting capacity refers to a parent's overall ability to parent the child across a range of needs, including basic care, safety, emotional warmth, stimulation, guidance/boundaries, stability, etc.). Parental capacity to change, on the other hand, is the range of attributes, capabilities, motivations and contextual factors etc. that may enable a parent to make changes for the benefit of the children, and to demonstrate that they can address critical difficulties that would otherwise have a detrimental impact on the child's welfare.

The C-Change approach draws on two particular academic developments based on theories of behaviour change (Platt & Riches, 2016a). The first came from the US, where a group of influential theorists were brought together to develop a common framework for understanding behaviour change – the unified theory of behaviour (described in Jaccard *et al*, 2002). The second came from an international collaboration that developed the Theoretical Domains Framework, which is aimed at using behaviour change and associated research in promoting change in a variety of professional contexts (Cane *et al*, 2012). Both approaches have their roots in a significant history of research and theory. The unified theory of behaviour is of particular relevance in the context of the present volume because it has been used in New York to support parents to meet their children's needs and to engage with mental health services where their children have mental difficulties. By applying the unified theory of behaviour, parent advocates could explore, alongside other factors, parental perceptions of what might be gained through engaging in treatment for their child, parental feelings of their own competence to support their child during treatment and the influence that their social norms may have (Olin *et al*, 2010).

In the C-Change approach, background theory is combined with an adaptation of Paul Harnett's work on assessing actual changes parents may make in the context of welfare concerns about their children (Harnett, 2007). The way in which these two aspects of the assessment are used is explained below.

Using C-Change

Availability of good quality assessment methods for practitioners to assess parental capacity to change is currently very limited. C-Change fills an important gap in this respect. After receiving training in the C-Change approach during the pilot project, one social worker commented:

*'I have never had it broken down like that before…
Never to break it down to being five domains like habits,
automatic responses, you know, all of those contextual
factors. I didn't have any framework to hang that on. So
it's helped massively.'*

C-Change focuses specifically on parental capacity to change. It is designed to be used alongside and integrated with standard methods of assessing children and their families, such as the *Framework for the Assessment of Children in Need, Signs of Safety*, or other equivalent approaches. For example, initially a children and families social work assessment might explore and identify any harm to the child and what parental actions or behaviours are thought to be responsible for this harm. An assessment of a parent's mental health status and how this affects their ability to meet their child's needs would also be undertaken, primarily as part of this wider children and families assessment. Information gathered about a parent's daily functioning and ability to process and understand the need for some changes would also be used to inform the analysis of capacity to change. All this information would then be used to inform the C-Change assessment.

C-Change may be used to assist decision-making when care proceedings are being considered; in decisions about not removing a child from parents where there is reasonable evidence that they should be able to continue with the child's care (with support); in planning to reunite children, who have been in care, with their parent(s) and in working with cases that appear to be 'stuck'. Research has identified that the process both of assessing and evidencing change can be lengthy (Harnett, 2007; Gardner, 2008) meaning the C-Change approach also has relevance for Early Help services. The C-Change approach aims to assist practitioners in understanding the complexities of the process of change and taking a holistic view of the factors that may be hindering parents in making changes. After undertaking the training practitioners often comment on an increased understanding of the interplay of the different factors affecting change, for example:

'It's huge [change]. And I think… Although I've been practicing for a long time, until I did this, I didn't actually sit down and actually think about it.'

Understanding

Basing the framework for this assessment on barriers to and facilitators of change was inspired by the behaviour change theories outlined above. This framework supports the practitioner in considering a range of factors including inherent motivational and related characteristics, as well as the context of wider problems that they may be facing. When parents have additional difficulties such as mental illness, we know that this can create significant challenges for them in meeting their children's needs consistently and protecting them from harm. It may also mean that changes they want to make for the benefit of their children can, in some cases, be significantly limited by the mental health conditions facing them, and the therapeutic regime available.

The importance of the C-Change approach in this context is that it encourages practitioners to examine the range of factors affecting change, not simply to assess the parents' mental health problems. Underpinning any assessment of capacity to change is the need for clarity about actual parental behaviours that have a detrimental impact on the child. These behaviours may or may not be affected by the parent's mental health. Rather than simply treating the mental health difficulties as the problem to be addressed, C-Change guides the practitioner to look at all of the factors affecting the likelihood of changing behaviours, positive as well as negative. In this way, practitioners can consider whether and how a parent's mental health is affecting their capacity to make changes. If a parent's mental health problems were not having a significantly harmful impact on the child, the problems would only be of interest, in a C-Change assessment, if they were preventing the parent from being able to change potentially harmful behaviours.

For example, one practitioner applied the framework of barriers and facilitators in thinking about the possible return from care of an adolescent who had been removed several years previously:

'When you've got structural, background disadvantages, mental health issues, possibly learning disability – when you've got those, it's hard for people to make decisions by themselves to make changes. It's helped in understanding what bits you can control and what bits you can't. What is it that's within her grasp and what isn't? How long will she be able to sustain it when other stresses come in e.g. money, housing? Structural things will affect her motivation or lack of motivation if you can't change some of that stuff.'

Another practitioner was working with a case where there was little progress as the parent was resistant to receiving interventions from Children's Services. By exploring the parent's barriers to engaging using the C-Change approach, the practitioner was able to help the parent overcome this barrier. As she commented in the evaluation:

'You might be thinking along the lines of, you know this parent can't do it because there's this thing that's really getting in the way of … this barrier that's really hindering her or him, because they can't see past that. And you … know that's a problem, but then [C-Change] helps you to think about why it's a problem, and what you might be able to do about it, and how big a problem is it.'

Action

The second component of C-Change, action, involves supporting parents to make real changes for the benefit of the children and measuring progress towards these changes. Specific behaviours that may be harming the child are identified, and intervention is offered to facilitate the necessary changes. Clear methods of assessment are included in the approach to help practitioners measure these changes. The technique of Goal Attainment Scaling is among the most promising of these methods, and provides a careful and thorough approach to setting goals and reviewing progress over an appropriate period of time.

This aspect of the assessment offers parents a 'live' opportunity to demonstrate their progress. It is of particular importance when dealing with parents with mental health difficulties. Rather than a potential over-reliance on what may be untested assumptions about how mental health difficulties may affect parenting, the approach gives parents a real opportunity, in carefully controlled circumstances, to demonstrate their capacity to address the problems. We know that the majority of parents with mental health problems do not cause significant harm to their children. In this approach, they get a chance to show whether or not their mental health difficulties are truly preventing them from addressing their child's needs.

The importance of using both aspects of the C-Change Approach

An example from one of the social workers involved in the pilot project provides a clear illustration of the benefit of using the framework of barriers and facilitators to understand the complexity of change and then testing this understanding by using the Goal Attainment Scaling method. The case involved a mother with long-standing mental health difficulties and her child who was currently in foster care, primarily due to emotional neglect linked to the mother's mental health. In exploring barriers and facilitators to change using the C-Change approach, this practitioner was able to look beyond the mother's mental health condition, which was unlikely to change significantly. She considered the current behaviours that were influenced by the mother's mental health and were negatively affecting her relationship with her child, but were amenable to intervention and, possibly, change. In this example, it was the mother's inconsistent presentation during contact that was causing continued concern for professionals, and harm to the child:

'What is getting in the way of positive contact is mum's mood on the day. If she's feeling positive, then contact will be positive, as he responds very well when she is positive. When she's not having a good day he picks up on that quite quickly, feeding the cycle of positivity. (The) thing that impacts massively on the contact is that cycle: (when) it's not consistent ..., he continues to have anxiety, and she continues to feel it won't always be positive.'

The Goal Attainment Scaling method was used to set goals with the mother around contact, and to measure whether she was able to make any changes. Using this method appeared to bring several benefits, including a shared agreement about what positive contact would be, and further information on what was preventing the mother's ability to change:

'Helped to define what 'positive contact' would actually look like... In conjunction with professionals and Mum – (we) wrote up ideas on the board so we had a very clear plan – Mum (was) able to contribute some ideas about what positive contact would look like but these were things that would make contact positive for her and not for the child, not in his best interests – again I was thinking, here is evidence of that lack of capacity to change. Quite a lot of clear information from that about what her priorities are, how much knowledge she has.'

This case provides an example of how using the C-Change approach can provide parents with meaningful and achievable goals to improve their ability to meet their child's needs based on a clear understanding of what needs to change and some

thinking about what might prevent a parent from making these changes. It encourages a respectful way of working that acknowledges a parent's mental health difficulties and the impact these have on their functioning and the child's experiences, without being constrained by the potentially slow pace of change in parental mental health.

Analysis

The C-Change approach guides practitioners through comparing and analysing the information gained from both elements, understanding and action, in relation to the assessed risk to the child. Consideration of the child's timescale (i.e. how quickly changes need to be made to ensure the child's developmental needs are met) is a fundamental aspect of this analysis.

The question, for the capacity to change element of an assessment, is what influence do the parents' characteristics or behaviours have on their capacity to make changes and to improve their ability to meet their children's needs? For example, a parent experiencing a borderline personality disorder may have automatic responses to attachment behaviours expressed by the child, and, for example, may demonstrate hostile or cold and unresponsive reactions to the child. Modifying habitual responses such as these is likely to require significant intervention and time.

Similarly, due to other personality traits, a parent might struggle to engage constructively in group settings, for example if they were offered a group-based parenting support programme. An exploration of this when considering parents for such a programme can avoid parents feeling that they have been 'set up to fail'.

The C-Change assessment is intended to help practitioners identify difficulties of this kind and to make decisions about how to address them. Thus, if problems of engaging constructively with their child could be overcome through some work on skills development, or difficulties of engaging with services could be addressed through appropriate counselling or providing an alternative intervention, the prospects for maintaining the child within the family (with appropriate support) would be enhanced. However, if the prospects for change are extremely limited and the potential for harm to the child if they remain in the family of origin is significant, initiating care proceedings may well be the appropriate course of action.

Evaluation of C-Change

C-Change was piloted in 2014-15 with three local authorities in South West England, and the C-Change manual (Platt & Riches, 2016b) was published in 2016, building on this experience. The pilot evaluation measured social workers' knowledge, skills and confidence in assessing parental capacity to change, using questionnaires applied before and after training, and at three-month follow-up. The results included statistically significant improvements in practitioner skills, knowledge and confidence; improvements in social workers' analyses in assessments; improved decision-making within the child's timescales, with potential avoidance of delay; reductions in the need for expert witnesses in court proceedings (in a small number of cases) and court reports well received by judges. One practitioner commented that:

'It offered a really good framework to … cement where those concerns [about capacity to change] sat in the assessment. I think without that sort of template, the social worker could likely find themselves stating things like, "my observations led me to believe da, da, da…", which of course when you're actually in court is sometimes upheld and other times not.'

Within three months of the training session, 87% of participants had been able to apply the C-Change approach in assessing families with whom they were working. This provides a clear indication that practitioners are willing and able to implement the C-Change approach in their practice.

Interest in C-Change is growing both in the UK and internationally. The University of Bristol has established a partnership with Interface Enterprises Ltd to provide training and support to local authorities who wish to embed the approach in practice.

Summary

The C-Change approach incorporates a relatively recent introduction of integrated theoretical approaches to behaviour change into assessments of children's welfare. It is intended to offer a rigorous approach to assessing parental capacity to change, an aspect of assessment that has often been neglected in the past. Initial evaluation suggests that it has good potential and it is the hope and intention of the authors of the approach to undertake further and more detailed evaluation in the near future.

References

Cane J, O'Connor D & Michie S (2012) Validation of the theoretical domains framework for use in behaviour change and implementation research. *Implementation Science* **7** 37.

Jaccard J, Dodge T & Dittus P (2002) Parent-adolescent communication about sex and birth control: a conceptual framework. *New Directions for Child and Adolescent Development* **97** 9–41.

Harnett P (2007) A procedure for assessing parents' capacity for change in child protection cases. *Children and Youth Services Review* **29** 1179–1188.

Gardner R (2008) *Developing an Effective Response to Neglect and Emotional Harm to Children* [online]. University of East Anglia & NSPCC. Available at: https://www.nspcc.org.uk/globalassets/documents/research-reports/developing-effective-response-neglect-emotional-harm-children.pdf (accessed June 2017).

Olin S, Hoagwood K, Rodriguez J, Ramos B, Burton G, Penn M & Jensen P (2010) The application of behaviour change theory to family-based services: improving parent empowerment in children's mental health. *Journal of Child and Family Studies* **19** (4) 462–470.

Platt D & Riches K (2016a) Assessing parental capacity to change: the missing jigsaw piece in the assessment of a child's welfare? *Children and Youth Services Review*, Volume 61, February 2016, pages 141–148.

Platt D & Riches K (2016b) *C-Change: Capacity to change assessment manual.* Bristol: University of Bristol.

Southwark parental mental health team

Reproduced with the kind permission of South London and Maudsley NHS Foundation Trust

The parental mental health team is a nurse led early intervention service, which works in Southwark to provide help and support for parents who have children under five and are experiencing mental illness. This service is commissioned by Southwark Council Children's service as part of their early help provision.

Chris McCree, Service Manager, has led the development of the team since it was set up in 2007. It was started as part of a drive to identify unmet needs in support provision for parents who have young children and are experiencing mental health problems.

The parental mental health team recognises the needs of parents as individuals with mental health problems, and the needs of the child. They aim to promote positive parenting and minimise the impact their mental health difficulties may have on their children through supporting the parents with their own needs. Service users are referred by a wide variety of professionals from different health services.

Chris said: 'The team provides both one-to-one and group sessions in children's centres. We therefore have a detailed knowledge of the interaction between parent and child which may not be immediately evident to other healthcare professionals. We see the family in their home environment and observe the interaction between the parent and child which is crucial to helping us develop the right care plan for the parent.'

Lucy Brazener, Team Manager, said: 'Some of our families really don't have very much; they may be struggling with benefits or have no recourse to public funds and by going into their homes we are able to identify what they need, for example, toys to stimulate the child or a fully working pushchair to make it easier for them to go out and thereby reducing isolation.'

In addition to the individual work the team runs a variety of therapeutic sessions. The 'keeping well post birth' group is a 10-week course that includes challenging negative thoughts and developing positive coping strategies as well as exploring feelings about motherhood. The team also runs a 'creative families' group, an art programme which aims to reduce the stigma of accessing mental health service and engages with families that are isolated. Through the medium of art it encourages parents to explore their mental well-being and to share their experiences. These sessions provide lunch and a crèche service, making it as easy as possible for parents to attend without having to worry about food or childcare.

The team will see parents with a range of mental health problems and they often work jointly with other community teams and children's services.

This service is available for any Southwark parent. For advice about how to refer, please contact lucy.brazener@southwark.gov.uk

'I'm so grateful to them for showing me I wasn't alone': Jane's story

'I first met Lucy and the team when my daughter was two, because I'd suffered with post-natal depression after my son was born a few years before. My daughter was a very difficult toddler, and used to scream the place down when we went out, simple things like getting on the bus became a nightmare. I stopped going out as much because of this so I became very isolated.

'Lucy took me to a children's centre where I did a parenting course. It was going to this I realised that there were other mothers in my situation. The sessions helped me build up my confidence, which was really very low. I also went with my daughter to stay and play sessions.

'What it took me a while to realise was that as my son was autistic, he'd never been a curious toddler. My daughter was completely different and was into everything which I wasn't used to so I thought there was something wrong with her. In actual fact she was completely fine.

'The sessions also showed me that I wasn't depressed like before, just really tired and down like most mothers get at some point or other. The parenting course taught me that I was actually a good enough parent after all that time I'd thought I was bad one.

'I was discharged from the care of the team but I still keep in touch with them as I actually talk to some of the groups now about my experience with postnatal depression and it's great to think that I might be helping others now. I've also managed to find a job and I'm so grateful to Lucy and the team at the children's centre for showing me I wasn't alone and for building up my confidence. It turned my life around.'

Pauline's interview

The following transcript is taken from an interview between Daphne McKenna – a member of the advisory group for this publication – and a parent who has used the service. Some small amendments have been made for clarity.
To listen to the interview, visit www.pavpub.com/ parental-mental-health-interviews/

Interviewer: I've got some questions that I'm going to ask you. Maybe we'll stick to them, maybe we won't, ok? But I really want to start by asking a bit about you and your family. So, how long have you been living at your address in Southwark?

Pauline: Since 2015. That's two years, and a couple of months.

Interviewer: Ok. So, who's in your family?

Pauline: My two boys and me.

Interviewer: Ok. What are the names and ages of your boys?

Pauline: My first one is George, he's ten years old and a half. And the last one is Kevin. He's four and a half.

Interviewer: So, what are they like?

Pauline: They are very lovely boys! And sometimes they have ups and downs. I love them so much because they're the only family I have in this country.

Interviewer: Ok. So, what sort of things are they interested in doing?

Pauline: My first boy likes football so much.

Interviewer: Which team does he support?

Pauline: Manchester United.

Interviewer: Of course.

Pauline: Yes (laughs). And the second boy, because he's too young, he's just following his brother around with football. But he knows nothing about football.

Interviewer: And what about you? Are you a fulltime mum or are you working?

Pauline: I'm a full-time mum.

Interviewer: And this may be a silly question, but do you get any spare time? And are there things that you like doing?

Pauline: Yes, sometimes when they are at school or when they are in bed I just sit down and watch movies.

Interviewer: Movies? That's interesting. Anything in particular?

Pauline: I like action movies.

Interviewer: Oh do you?

Pauline: Yes, because they are making [so] much noise. I don't like sad movies because they remind me sometimes of my past. I don't like it.

Interviewer: Ok, so you keep yourself happy by looking at action movies. So, is there anybody else? You say this is the only family you've got in this country. Are there other people around you that are important to you?

Pauline: Hmm, not exactly because the people that were important to me were professionals, like social services, like CAMHS, and the only person important to me now is Lucy because I prefer to trust professionals [over] friends.

Interviewer: Ok. And Lucy is the worker from the parental mental health service?

Pauline: Yes.

Interviewer: Tell me, when did you first come into contact with that service?

Pauline: I was with CAMHS regarding my first son. He was having some emotional problems, and I was pregnant with my last boy and they needed to refer me to Lucy's team.

Interviewer: So, can you tell me a little bit about what had led up to that? Why they felt you needed some help from this service?

Pauline: Yes, because of my condition and dealing with the children, the newborn, go out, meet people, because I was so… in me? Meet friends, talk about me. I know that some people like me have problems too.

Interviewer: Ok, so what happened? Did you have to come to them, or did they come to you? How did you first make contact?

Pauline: They had to come to me, because when CAHMS referred me to them, they had to come to me to tell me what's going on in the parenting mental health group *(inaudible)* what they're doing and what help they can get for me, which support I can have.

Interviewer: How did you feel about that? When they first arrived?

Pauline: I was feeling happy because, you know, like I said in the beginning, I don't like friends because professionals – I trust them, yes.

Interviewer: You mentioned Lucy before. Is Lucy your key worker?

Pauline: Yes, in parental mental health.

Interviewer: How long have you known her then? Has she been your key worker all the time?

Pauline: Yes, since four years – as soon as I gave birth to my little boy, yes.

Interviewer: When you first made contact, or they made contact with you, at this service, you were saying that you were struggling to cope with some of the demands on you of being a single parent. What was it like for your children?

Pauline: *(Inaudible)* My boy, he was asking about his dad, like to know who is the dad, and I didn't know how to explain that question. I was feeling sad. He was causing a lot of problems; at school, with friends, he became so aggressive, things like that. And it came out of the second pregnancy, how to cope after the birth. All this was in my mind.

Interviewer: So, am I right in thinking the two things were quite connected? How you were feeling was affecting your son?

Pauline: Yes.

Interviewer: And how your son was feeling was affecting you?

Pauline: Yes.

Interviewer: And you said that you'd got involved with CAHMS (child and adolescent mental health service); were there any other professionals in your life at the time, or any other sources of support?

Pauline: Yes! Social services – children's social services – and mental health *(inaudible)*.

Interviewer: You had a community psychiatric nurse for you?

Pauline: Yes.

Interviewer: Ok, before this service?

Pauline: Yes.

Interviewer: So, tell me a bit about *this* service and what did they do that has helped you? Describe it for me?

Pauline: They helped me a lot to understand life; how to show love to my newborn child; how to play with him; how to cope with him; with all those things I was having in my mind. And holiday and Lucy, and I, sorry I didn't go to her because she was very nice worker and she supported me a lot. On holiday she we could come to my house and we'd go out to the park with the children because I was finding it a little bit difficult with the baby and his brother. We'd go out. Sometimes we'd go to the theatre; we'd go to the park; picnic.

Interviewer: You're making it sound as if she did a lot of very practical things, but also things that were fun, to help you.

Pauline: Yes.

Interviewer: And did you do that as a family or did she just see *you*? Was anybody working with the children?

Pauline: No, no, because I was not alone, because there was a lot in the group, not just the only one, but with the other mothers and the children.

Interviewer: So you took part in the group activities that Lucy had organised?

Pauline: Yes.

Interviewer: What was is like meeting other parents in a similar situation?

Pauline: Yeah, it was nice. At least when we would go we would share problems, because we had similar problems.

Interviewer: So I'm assuming your eldest boy was at school a lot of that time, but the baby, your youngest son, came with you?

Pauline: Yes.

Interviewer: Do you think there were any benefits for your older boy?

Pauline: Yes, because there was organised events in the break, like *(inaudible)*, my son loves that day and still remembers it today. They have fun; they play with fire; they went to the fire station. He was very happy. Very happy.

Interviewer: This is a difficult question, but thinking back over that time, what did you do for yourself to build on the work that was being done by the team?

Pauline: Listened to their advice, and trust them, because the eldest listened to me but *(inaudible)* because with her I always work, yes, *(inaudible)* if you have any kind of difficulties or maybe anything, boredom of mind, problem with the children or something, I'm free to call her or, before, my English is too small, I need to find ways to go and see her so we could have a talk face-to-face. But now I can speak English I can try and talk very well – if I have any difficulties I can call her on the phone and she'll advise me on the phone and maybe try and find ways to come and see me at home.

Interviewer: So, you're describing some very supportive things that Lucy did, but also she had made it possible for you to trust her so that you could share your worries with her, and you're describing also getting a lot of benefit from meeting other parents in the group. I don't want to put words in your mouth, but is it like, knowing that other people had similar experiences was helpful?

Pauline: Yes.

Interviewer: Were there any other things that maybe other people were doing for you at that same time that helped?

Pauline: Yes, CAHMS. They helped my son to understand that there are children out there who live just with the mum, no daddy, and they're doing very well. And it took time for him to understand that bit, but now he understands that. And it took me time to understand that I'm not the only single mother to look after children; that a lot of single mothers look after children, and…

Interviewer: And they cope alright.

Pauline: Yeah.

Interviewer: Was there anything else that was happening at that time that was helpful?

Pauline: Regarding children's services, they supported me a lot with the two children; support financially and because children's services referred me to all those groups like CAMHS and all those groups.

Interviewer: So they sort of started it off for you and put you in touch with this service. Tell me, would you recommend this service to other people?

Pauline: Yes!

Interviewer: If you were recommending it to somebody else, what would you tell them? If you were trying to explain to me, and persuade me, how would you persuade me?

Pauline: I would recommend them to those people that are lonely, like me. I would recommend them because they made me understand that there are people in this life like me. They made me understand that I need to move on with life. They made me understand that those children are special to me.

Interviewer: That's a really nice recommendation. Before we finish, is there anything else you want to say about this service or about anything else that's helped you and your family?

Pauline: Yes, it was very helpful to me because when I remember where I come from and where I am now, and I can sit down in front of someone and speak, they're doing a great job. And I don't know, like, African ladies always say, God bless the service, or, I don't know how to put it, or the parental mental [health service] because they do a lot of good work, and especially me, Pauline, I thank so much because when I see my children today and me, myself, and I'm doing well with them, I just say thank you.

Lucy's interview

The following transcript is taken from an interview between Daphne McKenna – a member of the advisory group for this publication – and Lucy Brazener, the team manager of Southwark's Parental Mental Health team. To watch a video of the interview, visit www.pavpub.com/parental-mental-health-interviews/

Interviewer: So Lucy, thanks for agreeing to meet me. I'm interested in talking to you about Southwark's parental mental health team; find out a bit about when it started, why it started, and really to hear about some of your successes, not just in terms of the parent but in terms of the whole family. So, when was the service set up, and why?

Lucy: So, the service first started back in 2007. It came out of the Southwark *mental health family strategy*, which I think started about 2005. And it came out, there'd been several serious incidents within Southwark at that time that involved two child deaths, so it was really about doing something different at that time. So the team was set up to bridge that gap between adult mental health and children, and CAMHS.

Interviewer: The crossover?

Lucy: Yeah, the crossover into working in a way that thought about the family as a whole and young children.

Interviewer: So, who's in the team? How many of you are there?

Lucy: So, there's myself, I'm a community mental health nurse, and then we have two other full-time staff – we've got another community mental health nurse and an occupational therapist. And then we have a part-time occupational therapist who works two days a week, and two support practitioners who share a full time post. So, not a huge team.

Interviewer: So a range of disciplines but quite a small team?

Lucy: Yeah. We're a nurse-led service, so we don't have any medical cover.

Interviewer: So, how long have you been the manager?

Lucy: Since about 2011. So, I joined the team in 2009.

Interviewer: And, er, this is a bit of a tricky question, but what attracted you to this post of being team manager?

Lucy: I guess it was the flexibility in the way of working; being able to do early intervention; being able to work with the family as a whole; being out and about actively in the community and building up those partnerships, not just with families but with the services that parents accessed.

Interviewer: Tell me a bit about who, exactly, is eligible for this service.

Lucy: Anybody with children under the age of five that is a parent or the primary carer. They have to be experiencing some sort of mental distress to access the service. People can usually come on a referral from health visitors, GPs, children centre staff – any sort of professional who comes into contact with young families. We do occasionally take self-referrals as well.

Interviewer: That's very flexible! So, do you have a waiting list?

Lucy: No. So, we try to see people within four to six weeks, so we're not a crisis service in that sense, and if there were more, greater risk issues then obviously we can co-work with community mental health teams.

Interviewer: And is your involvement with families time-limited?

Lucy: No, er, so we can be quite flexible with that as well.

Interviewer: That's incredibly flexible. And, again, I don't know if you have a protocol around it but if you finish a piece of work with a family and their situation changes, are they able to come back into the service?

Lucy: Yeah, so we've had people come back. Perhaps there's been another crisis or something else has presented in their life, and they're still eligible for the service because they still have a child under the age of five, or perhaps they've gone on and had another child. So yeah, people do come back into the service sometimes.

Interviewer: Tell me a little bit about the sort of service you provide here. What range of things go on?

Lucy: So, we always see parents in the home – we recognise it's really difficult to get out of the house when you've got young families. So we see people in the home; we do a mental health needs assessment in context with their role of parenting, and then we'll offer them individual or group work depending on what their needs are, depending on what they need at that time, and what they would like. We also help people access other local services: maybe they're children's centre services; it may be a referral into therapy, or doing the preparation work – sometimes people aren't quite ready yet, so it's to help prepare them for the steps to therapy. So it really does depend, it's a wide variety of things that can be offered.

Interviewer: It's a really important point though, isn't it, about actually helping people prepare for some of the services? A lot of people sort of shy away from them and actually that encouragement and understanding about it is important.

Lucy: Yeah, and if you've had a poor relationship with services in the past, sometimes it's about building that trust up with people so that they then feel able to access services.

Interviewer: Could you give me an example of the sorts of... well I suppose there's no such thing as a typical case... but an example?

Lucy: Erm, well when I first started working with the team I worked with a lady who had an older autistic son who was high functioning, but she then had a little girl who, when it came to managing her tantrums, it became quite difficult because she'd been used to managing her autistic child.

Actually, to then see a normal child development was quite tricky for her. So, part of the work was about normalising her daughter's behaviour. She was a lady who had a long history of depression; it was about building up her confidence as a parent, and part of that was about her attending a local parenting course as well.

Interviewer: So partly about building on her strengths?

Lucy: Yeah, building on her strengths and looking at coping strategies she could use.

Interviewer: You talk about the service being for the whole family… Do you work with the children at all?

Lucy: I suppose we work with children in the sense that we'll think about their needs. So, although primarily it's the adult that's our patient, we will consider the impact of the parent's difficulties on the rest of the family. So, for example, we might have a parent that's been referred to us who is lonely, post-birth; they might have some history of trauma and are struggling with those early days of parenthood. So some of that may be, for example, a referral to parent-infant therapy so they can work that in a therapeutic and containing way.

Interviewer: You said before that you're quite a small team. What's the sort of average number of families you can work with at any one time?

Lucy: People's caseloads are around 20-25, and I guess you know there is movements because some people we will see for just a couple of sessions, some people stay with us for a lot longer. It's just dependent on the need, but ideally what we want to do is build up their own support network so they are then resilient to go back into the community and to use the existing services.

Interviewer: So, I don't know, do you have figures on how many families you might have helped across a year? Does that make sense?

Lucy: It does, it's a really good question. I can tell you that I think the team's caseload currently is probably about 120 families, something like that. And some of those families will be doing the group work as well.

Interviewer: So, what would you say, or can you give me some examples, of things that you think are real successes that you think have been achieved by this team because of the model, the framework that you use?

Lucy: Yeah, I think we've built up a really good relationship with children's centres; I think although we're a small team we cover the whole borough. We are well known throughout the children's centres. So I think that partnership working has been really important. I think the group work that we do: so for example, we do the 'keeping well post-birth' group; it's a ten-week psycho-educational programme; it runs one morning a week in a children's centre; the babies go into the crèche, and the mothers do the group programme. But also, you know, we invite other people in, so they have a psychologist come in, a child psychotherapist come in… So

I think that's been a really successful group, and that's been running several years now. And we do the creative families so I think our partnership with arts and health is something that I'm very proud of. That, again, is a ten-week programme; it runs in partnership with South London gallery and the local children's centres. The first five weeks are the parents in the children's centres doing an activity with an artist. They have a member of our team and a member of the gallery present as well, and the children are in the crèche. And then the second five weeks are the parents and the children going to the gallery and then doing a series of art workshops together as well. And we presented that at AESOP (Arts Enterprise with a Social Purpose) … so we presented that last year as an example of good practice between arts and health as well. So that's been formally evaluated – I mean, both groups have.

Interviewer: Speaking to someone who's used your service, I notice that you do a lot of fun things as well. Tell me a bit about those.

Lucy: So, the fun things that we do, I think it's recognising that parenting is a tough job. If you're experiencing mental health difficulties sometimes you need sometimes you need those positive moments to keep you going. So, in the holidays we'll always try to run a picnic, or we'll do the trip to the fire station, which was a while ago, but it's just thinking about things that we can do – the Christmas toy campaign we've been running for a few years now, so that, especially those families on low incomes, or for whatever reason just don't have the financial resources, that actually there is something they can give their children at Christmas.

Interviewer: You've also mentioned that you do individual work but you do group work. In your opinion what are the benefits of group work? Is it just to see more people or are there other intrinsic benefits?

Lucy: I think the benefits are that people don't feel like they're alone; I think the power is being in the group itself, and I think sometimes people can say things that perhaps a professional couldn't. So I think it's a lot to do with the power of the group and feeling that you're not the only who feels that way – that actually there are other parents feeling the same.

Interviewer: Do you think that people maintain friendships or networks once their time with the service is finished?

Lucy: I know from the groups that people do sometimes still link up, and people sometimes form friendships. I can't say that about every group because every group's dynamic is slightly different, but I know there's certainly been groups where that's happened.

Interviewer: Ok, you talked a bit about the benefits for parents of group work and some of the contacts, the networks, that they maintain. Can you tell me a bit about, from your experience, whether you've seen benefits for the children of this service?

Lucy: So I think the benefit to the children is that the parents are beginning to have conversations with their children about their mental health difficulties and the impact that it's had, or their concerns about when they're feeling a bit sad, and what's that about. I think it's also about strengthening their relationship, having those positive experiences, and about strengthening their relationship with their child, and being able to access services – not just for them but also for their child. I think that's really important.

Interviewer: I want to change tack slightly now and talk a little bit about your team. What supports and sustains you as a team to continue carrying out this work. I mean, what do you need to function as you do?

Lucy: Erm, I think, although we're out and about in the community quite a lot I think we're actually quite a close team, and I think everybody who's in the team feels very passionate about what we do. I think, you know, you can see the impacts within families, and I think we still meet regularly, we still have regular clinical team meetings, we have regular supervision... We have all those sorts of governance in place still, but I think it's also really about having that shared interest in working within this way and being able to be that flexible in approach. Because, you know, you might be in the north of the borough in the morning and then in the afternoon you're in the south, and I think it's about being able to manage the travelling and that uncertainty as well. So I think you have to manage quite a lot, and I think the team do it in a way that's very successful.

Interviewer: You said earlier that your service is quite well known. How does Southwark manage to do that? Do you feel that you've got the support of the organisation?

Lucy: Which organisation? The trust, or the...

Interviewer: Both really... I mean, how do you work?

Lucy: I think locally we certainly have that support. I think we're very fortunate that over the years we've built up relationships with children's centres, with the local community mental health team, with children's social care. So we are well known and if people don't know about us then they soon will because quite often we will work in partnership with other services. So if you're having a 'team around the family' meeting that's another way to get to know about the service, and health visitors obviously know us, and I think one of the challenges is when you have turnover of staff in other services you have to continually promote your service. So it is continuously about going out there, meeting the other services, letting them know that you're still here, and doing events and ... doing talks on the team, being at events and just saying yes to most things that we're asked to do.

Interviewer: So, what about you? What sustains you in this role? What do you draw on?

Lucy: I really enjoy doing this work, because I've been doing it for such a long time now and I think it's very poignant that I was, very early on in my nursing career, on an acute ward and I cared for one of the parents who was part of that serious case review right in the very beginning. So I think if you can

do something differently and there's a chance to intervene early, why wouldn't you? It's a bit of a no-brainer, I think, really.

Interviewer: There's a lovely circularity.

Lucy: Yeah, and also you just never want to repeat the mistakes of the past. I think it's about an opportunity to do something differently and to work in a way that offers the flexibility to families that is meeting their needs.

Interviewer: And to truly learn (inaudible).

Lucy: Yeah, and I think, going back to the other question about the team, the team has quite a strong sense of learning, and so you know, training... Our two support workers, for example, have done post-graduates in family work. So, you know, we have a strong sense in education and training for us so we can go out there and be as skilled as we can be. And improving practise and outcomes.

Interviewer: So tell me a little about your relationship with the partner agencies. How easy is it to work with other partner agencies on board?

Lucy: I think it's probably been quite easy. I think it's about how you go out and present yourself to people; I think it's about not being defensive; it's about going and being open and transparent, and if something hasn't been done helpfully in the past, how can we change that and make things better? So how can we improve on building that partnership?

Interviewer: Do you see any changes to practice in the partner agencies as a result of your input? Anything different?

Lucy: I think that's a hard question to answer. I mean, I'd like to think that people are – especially from other services and from mental health – are able to think more in a 'think family' way... The other thing the team will do is that we sometimes do teaching sessions on basic mental health awareness, for example for children's centre staff, so if they're picking up that someone's a bit tearful, feeling a bit low, actually they know where to refer that person to, or they know who to speak to for advice. So I'd like to think that perhaps people are thinking more about where families can access help. So that they're not having to hold so much, and actually we can hold it together.

Interviewer: Has there ever been any evaluation of the service that your team provides?

Lucy: Yeah, so all the groups we run have been evaluated and we've just finished undertaking a service evaluation. I think one of the things that we find very tricky is getting people to do pre- and post-clinical questionnaires. People's lives are very chaotic, it doesn't necessarily always feel... well, it's not always the right time when someone's in crisis to then say, 'Can you fill out a form?' English, for a lot of our families, is not their first language – a lot of clinical questionnaires tend to be written for people in an English-language speaking culture. So I think there's lots of challenges. I think the way forward is to perhaps get a small group of people and do more narratives, and get the quality from the data that way, so I think that would be the next step really, for the team.

Interviewer: From the information that you do have, what would you say are the key outcomes? You know, the measures of success? You know, could you sum those up in some way?

Lucy: I think the key outcomes are about improvements in people's mental health. Thinking about the child I think they're the sort of key outcomes. And then thinking about how we move forward with that, you know, in terms of reducing parental stress, because I think one of the things is that you build a relationship up with someone but then they start telling you more things that they need help with. So sometimes people's stresses go up rather than down because they're beginning to disclose more things.

Interviewer: Because they've got that relationship?

Lucy: And they've got that relationship – yeah. Because that's the other thing about the team, it's building that trusting relationship with people.

Interviewer: Looking ahead to the future, how do you see the future of this team? How do think things are going to pan out? Or, if that's too difficult a question, how would you *like* them to pan out?

Lucy: I would like the team to continue to be funded. I think it's invaluable the work the team does; I think we are valued by the partnerships we have; I think it's recognising the impact that if you get in early, either [in terms of the] age of the child or at the early point of the parent's mental health difficulties, actually the impact that can have is far greater, potentially, although slightly harder to measure, on the family as a whole in improving outcomes. And it'd be great to do a greater in-depth service evaluation. To replicate the team, would be great, in other boroughs.

Interviewer: So, before we finish, is there anything else you want to say about the way in which your team works? The service that you provide? Anything you haven't yet covered?

Lucy: I don't know… Just the team work really hard! And it's not just about the group work – it's about the individual work; it's about getting people to think about their coping strategies; it's talking to their partners, you know, bringing *them* in; thinking about the older children as well, not just the younger ones that are in the home, because, you know, think about young carers and their role in the families and how sometimes they can be missed.

Interviewer: So truly trying to take a 'whole-family' approach?

Lucy: Yes. And I think … we're in the process of building on the Southwark Family Strategy so there is a trust-wide one for SLAM[1].

Interviewer: Before we close, is there anything else that you'd like to add about the work that's done by this team? Your successes? Anything that helps you continue to function?

Lucy: Well, I guess it's that thinking that it's cost-effective in the long term to work in this way – to do early intervention with families, either at the early point of the parent's difficulties or the age of a child. And I think it's about recognising how hard the team work to engage families by going out and assertively knocking on their doors. And I guess also we owe a huge amount to Chris McKree who essentially set up our service, who's been instrumental in the Southwark mental health family strategy and in promoting a 'think family' approach throughout Southwark and I know she's spread the word across the world as well, going to international conferences. So yeah, without her the team wouldn't exist, so I think we have a lot to be thankful to Chris for…

---

1 South London and Maudsley NHS Trust.

Creative Families Art Programme

Lucy Brazener and Heather Kay

Creative Families is an early intervention arts programme for parents experiencing mental health difficulties and their children aged under five years. Creative Families aims to help vulnerable families in an inner city area to promote mental well-being by engaging them in a series of artist-led workshops, and developing a replicable programme. It runs in partnership with the Southwark Parental Mental Health Team (PMHT), South London Gallery (SLG) and local children's centres. Funding was awarded by Guy's and St Thomas' Charitable Trust for a two-year service evaluation, which began in 2013 and enabled six Creative Families' programmes to be run over two years with 46 parents and 61 children participating.

The Creative Families programme had the following clinical health outcomes for parents:

→ Reduced feelings of stress and anxiety.

→ Improved mood.

→ Increased confidence.

→ Reduced feelings of social isolation.

→ Promoted positive engagement and attachment between parent and child.

→ Promoted the emotional, social and cognitive development of the child.

To promote social inclusion and overcome the stigma of accessing mental health services, the Creative Families programme is held in two venues – a local children's centre and the SLG – and runs one morning a week for 10 weeks. The programme is held during term time with the first five weeks in a local children's centre with crèche provision, while the parents engage in artist-led workshops. There is a break in half term followed by five weeks held in the SLG with parents and their children participating together.

Current funding for the programme has been secured from within the PMHT budget.

Description of the arts activity

The artists commissioned for Creative Families are all experienced in socially engaged art practice and are able to work skillfully with a group, which requires sensitivity to group dynamics and individual needs, and an awareness of the boundaries laid out by professional guidelines regarding working with vulnerable people. Artists commissioned for the service evaluation programmes were Davina Drummond, Lawrence Bradby, Daniel Lehan and Jessica Scott.

Following are some examples of artists' work in the programme:

→ Davina Drummond's practice is concerned with craft, motherhood, and the process of making. The sessions used print-making, text and fabric to explore participant's feelings through experiences of making alongside others. Feelings of imperfection were explored through making and dealing with imperfections. Participants also made something to physically take home: a calendar or stamp with their own positive mantra, which they could keep as a reminder from the sessions. To ensure participants could replicate activities at home, all materials used were affordable.

→ Bradby's (of Townley and Bradby) sessions focused on learning to think about domestic space and the challenges of parenthood in a playful way. A wide range of playful activities were used, such as drawing, arranging domestic objects and transforming them, playing games and storytelling. The activities enabled parents to reconnect with their own playfulness while sharing their feelings of everyday parenting. Activities with parent and child focused on child-led play. A digital camera was available for participants to take pictures of the activities, and during the project the photos were displayed as a tool to reflect on previous sessions.

→ Daniel Lehan's practice records and celebrates everyday happenings through hand-written text, often drawing on chance conversations. His workshops drew out parents' own stories, hopes and aspirations, which they then explored through typography. This involved using stencils and handwriting to create artwork around emotionally significant words and phrases, which enabled participants to share their own experiences and feelings around parenting and cultural differences.

→ Jessica Scott's work uses domesticity and the home as a form of universal understanding and a way of connecting with others. Her work draws from feminism to explore, re-affirm and reclaim what can be seen as typically feminine crafts and skills. She shared her quilt-making practice with the group, and explored these crafts with a focus on social activism. She facilitated activities such as adding calligraphy to crockery, writing on tea towels and producing a collective quilt. She incorporated a focus on using recycled and cheap materials, so that participants would learn to be creative by producing work at very low cost.

Project participants

Parents are referred to the programme by the PMHT through the Common Assessment Framework (CAF) from a wide range of statutory and non-statutory services, such as health visiting, children's social care, children's centres and adult mental health services. All parents referred to the PMHT have children aged under five and are experiencing mental health difficulties, for example depression and/or anxiety, and are seen at home for a mental health needs assessment before joining the group.

All participants give signed consent to the CAF on referral to the PMHT, and participation is voluntary. Informed consent is sought from the PMHT before commencing Creative Families. All participants receive a copy of the treatment plan for Creative Families in accordance with local mental health trust policy on data protection and confidentiality. Artists do not therefore blog or upload images of participants on social media or anywhere online.

Project management

The delivery team for the workshops consists of the artist, the SLG community projects manager and the adult mental health practitioner.

All parents that participate in the programme are under the care of the PMHT and the adult mental health practitioner provides emotional support in the session and encourages attendance by sending a text reminder before each session. Additional home visits and phone calls are offered by the adult mental health practitioner if the parents require further support due to any crises that may emerge while participating in the programme.

The community projects manager is responsible for commissioning artists who have previous experience in participatory arts for each programme, encouraging reflection and mentoring for artists that are early on in their career.

The artist is responsible for planning each session, as well as leading on the creative activity and participation. The artist also engages in post-session reflection with the adult mental health practitioner and community projects manager, who completes a reflection log for each session.

Evaluation methods and findings

The Creative Families pilot project was evaluated through an innovative partnership between the South London and Maudsley Trust Centre for Parent and Child Support, and Goldsmiths, University of London, Centre for Urban and Community Research. The service evaluation used a mixed method approach and the final reports reflect the differences in evaluation methods, which can be read together in *Making it Together*, which can be obtained from: http://www.southlondongallery.org/page/creativefamilies

In summarising some of the health outcomes, pre- and post-scores of the participants scored showed that there was a 77% reduction in their depression and anxiety scores and 86% reduction in stress using the Depression, Anxiety, Stress and Scale (DASS). Participants also reported an 80% reduction in their child's primary problem using the Brief Infant Toddler Social and Emotional Assessment (BITSEA). Participant feedback was that the programme provided an opportunity to learn and try new ways of interacting with their child and helped increase confidence to access other services within the community, while having a mental health practitioner present in the group was a helpful and positive experience.

There was a great deal of inter-sectoral learning from Creative Families in terms of arts and health working together. For example in delivering the programme, there was an increased understanding of each other's roles and responsibilities, which has been to the benefit of the programme. This learning has been shared at conferences nationally, with the teams co-presenting their findings.

Following the pilot, funding from the mental health team was secured to enable the project to continue with one ten-week project a year. In the autumn of 2016, artist Oriana Fox led a project with a live-art focus. This was a new direction for the programme and provided a different approach for the parents to problem-solve difficulties in their daily lives. Activities included role-play, freeze-frames, games and music sharing, which enabled parents to share their personal experiences in a light-hearted way.

Specialist roles and responsibilities

Northern Ireland Champions Initiative

Mary Donaghy, Gavin Davidson and Sharon Crawford

Introduction

Northern Ireland was one of six implementation sites for the Social Care Institute of Excellence's *Think Child, Think Parent, Think Family* guidance (SCIE, 2009). While the Northern Ireland implementation site ended in October 2012, it became 'core business' for the Health & Social Care Board (HSCB) under the structure of the well-established Children & Young Peoples Strategic Partnership (CYPSP) as an existing Regional Sub Group (for more information, see www.cypsp.org/regional-subgroups/think-family).

Now known as 'Think Family Northern Ireland' (TFNI), it has developed a regional action plan based on the three main themes that arose from the outcome of the Think Family 'Experience' Survey Report, which explored the views of service users, carers and staff (Donaghy, 2016).

The three themes were:

→ improve communication and information sharing between professionals and families

→ improve access to early intervention family support for children, young people and their families

→ improve the extent to which assessment, planning and treatment is inclusive of a 'whole family' approach.

(Donaghy, 2016)

Figure1 highlights the current work areas and initiatives being developed as core business (Phase two) for the HSCB under TFNI and we are continuing to use *The Family Model Handbook* (Falkov, 2012) as the framework for improving family focused practice within Northern Ireland.

However, the development of the Champions Initiative, which is just one of the work areas outlined in the diagram and is currently underway within four of the local Health & Social Care Trusts, follows this initiative having already been developed within the Northern Health & Care Trust (NHSCT) from 2009. It was now time to expand this initiative to the other trust areas following the evaluation of NHSCT Champions by Queen's University, Belfast.

Figure 1: Phase Two   Think Family Initiatives Northern Ireland

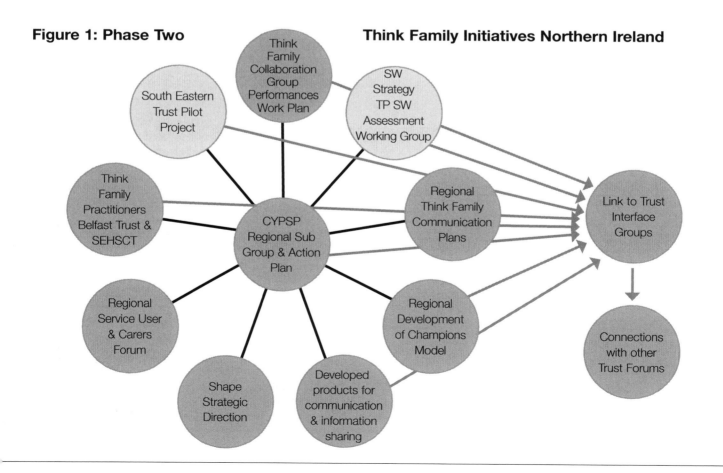

Champions Initiative

The Champions Initiative, which was piloted in one health and social care trust area starting in 2009, was a direct result of the O'Neill Inquiry (Independent Inquiry Panel to the Western and Eastern Health and Social Services Boards, 2008). This inquiry highlighted a number of issues, including poor communication between professionals, lack of information sharing, lack of communication with the patients' families, the need for training and education for adult mental health staff, and the interface between adult mental health and children's services.

The SCIE guidance, meanwhile, had included the recommendation that local 'champions' should be identified with 'specific responsibility for ensuring that recommendations are implemented' (SCIE, 2009, p36). This recommendation referred to the need for senior managers to lead change, but the pilot in Northern Ireland involved champions in each of the relevant adult mental health and child protection teams instead. It is now planned to implement this approach across all of the health and social care trusts in Northern Ireland.

In this chapter the general development of the role of champions will be considered; the context and implementation of the pilot Champions Initiative will be outlined; the findings of the evaluation of that pilot will be examined; and the plans to further implement this approach across Northern Ireland will be discussed.

The use of champions to promote change

An early meaning of the term 'champion' perhaps still conveys some sense of the potential strengths and limitations of this role. Traditionally, a champion would have been one of your best soldiers or knights who would have gone into single combat to represent a whole army. However, given the limits of mediaeval conflict resolution, it was usually still necessary for the whole army to engage with the issue.

In the 1960s, the role of a champion that would lead innovation and change in organisations was developed. In one of the seminal texts on this subject, Donald Schon, himself a champion of reflective practice, suggested that:

'... where radical innovation is concerned, the emergence of a champion is required. Given the underground resistance to change ... the new idea either finds a champion or dies...' (Schon, 1963, p84)

Schon argued that:

→ new ideas tend to encounter resistance

→ overcoming that resistance requires a lot of energy

→ support for change often comes through informal processes

→ and a champion tends to emerge who leads the process.

(Greenhalgh et al, 2005).

The need to address the process of change has become increasingly accepted in health and social care (Iles & Sutherland, 2001). This has been reinforced by the growing literature on 'implementation science', or how to more effectively introduce and implement evidence based developments in health and social care (Cabassa, 2016).

Warrick (2009, p15) defined the role of champion in this context and identified its three key roles: 'A change champion can be defined as a person at any level of the organisation who is skilled at initiating, facilitating, and implementing change'. Shaw et al (2012) detailed the various behaviours and skills required in order to fulfil the role of champion successfully:

'... actively and enthusiastically promoting a new innovation; making connections between different people in the organisation; mobilising resources; navigating the socio-political environment inside the organisation; building support for the innovation by expressing a compelling vision and boosting organisational members' skills and confidence; and ensuring that the innovation is implemented in the face of organisational inertia or resistance.' (p676)

Shaw et al also usefully distinguish between two different types of champion – those who lead a specific project and those who lead more general change across the whole organisation. They argue that the ideal combination is to have project champions and organisational change champions working closely together.

It is therefore important to acknowledge that the use of champions is only one aspect of how evidence-based approaches can be implemented in practice. In their systematic review of the research on this process, or implementation science as it has been more recently called, Braithwaite et al (2014) identified eight factors that have been demonstrated to be important:

→ Preparing for change.

→ Having people with the capacity for implementation.

→ Having settings with the capacity for implementation.

→ The types of implementation.

→ Resources.

→ Leverage, including the use of champions.

→ Positive processes, like communication and evaluation, which enable implementation.

→ Sustainability.

As the change management literature repeatedly reinforces, in addition to considering these positive components of change, it is also important to respond to the potential obstacles and restraining forces that may be relevant (Iles & Sutherland, 2001). The National Institute of Clinical Excellence (NICE, 2007) identified a number of types of barriers to change, including: awareness and knowledge; motivation; acceptance and beliefs; skills; practicalities; and barriers in the external environment, which may be beyond our control.

It is also important to clarify that the intention of champions is not that they, and they alone, implement change – their role is to lead and facilitate the relevant change for all those who are involved. Hendy and Barlow (2012), in their examination of the implementation of 'telecare' found that champions may be more useful in initial phases but could also potentially become a barrier to the later embedding and sustaining processes. They caution 'against allowing change to become positioned within the remit of a few individuals. Whilst this strategy may be initially beneficial, the role of champion may be less useful, even detrimental to progress, in the later stages of implementation.' (p348)

A final caveat, from Greenhalgh et al (2005) who reviewed the evidence for innovation in health care, is that research evidence on change tends to focus on the specific project under scrutiny and then make connections between that project and whatever changes are observed, whereas in these complex organisations and contexts there may be a much broader range of variables that may have contributed to both the success and limitations of change projects.

Development of the Champions Initiative in Northern Ireland

Health and social care was integrated in Northern Ireland by the Health and Personal Social Services Order 1972. This was partly in response to concerns about sectarianism in local government but it was also motivated by the desire to have a more systemic and holistic approach to care (Campbell et al, 2013). Integrated structures alone, however, do not resolve all interface issues and, leading up to the implementation of the pilot, difficulties with the interface between adult mental health and child protection services were identified. The Social Services Inspectorate's (2006) inspection of child protection services found that there 'is a need, at all levels, for more effective interagency strategies for responding to alcohol and drug misuse, mental health problems and domestic violence and their impact on children and young people' (p8). The panel of one inquiry, which followed the tragic death of a mother and her daughter, reported that it 'was particularly concerned that so many staff working in the field of adult mental health were clearly unaware of their responsibilities in relation to Child Protection Policies and Procedures and Children in Need Procedures' (Independent Inquiry Panel to the Western and Eastern Health and Social Services Boards, 2008, p7).

In one Trust area, there had been some early work on the interface between adult and children's services that had identified a number of issues including lack of information sharing, poor role clarity, and poor communication and resources. Based on that work it was suggested that a worker – a champion – could be identified in each of the relevant mental health and child protection teams to facilitate interface working. The Champions Initiative therefore started in January 2009 and was evaluated as part of the Think Family Initiative.

What is the role of a champion within adult mental health and children's services?

The role of a champion within adult mental health and children's services is:

→ to take a lead role in the team on the interface between mental health and child care

→ to create greater awareness of the impact of mental health conditions on parenting and childhood experiences.

Their tasks are:

→ To be lead champion within their own team.

→ To raise issues at team discussions.

→ To share learning with team members.

→ To provide advice to team members.

→ To promote joint working.

→ To contribute to local training initiatives.

→ To identify obstacles to better co-operation.

The competences for child care champion in mental health include the following:

→ Recognise child abuse, know regional child protection procedures.

→ Understand the case conference process.

→ Understand child care assessments used in children's services and the single point of access teams for referrals into children's services.

→ Understand the implications of mental illness on parenting.

→ Have knowledge of relevant inquiries.

→ Have experience of co-working cases with child care.

The competences for mental health champion in child care include the following:

→ Have a basic knowledge of mental illness and be able to recognise poor mental health.

→ Understand multi-disciplinary working and the role of community mental health teams.

→ Understand the implications of mental illness on parenting.

→ Have knowledge of relevant inquiries.

→ Have experience of co-working cases with mental health staff.

Evaluation of the Champions Initiative pilot

The evaluation that followed the initiative involved collecting data and using questionnaires from the champions and their team members at baseline, and from the champions and their team leaders at a six month follow-up. The evaluation was written up in more detail by Davidson et al (2012) but the findings at baseline reinforced the fact that the teams were encountering the complex issues identified in the SCIE guidance (2009).

The six month follow-up, which focused on impact, suggested there had been:

'... a positive impact on professionals' awareness, identification and discussion of the issues, and also of how these are communicated and referred across the interface. The reasons for the positive impact reported by the Champions may include the clear identification of someone at the front-line to take responsibility for identifying any difficulties with interface working, within and between the teams they are working with, and addressing those.' (p168)

As acknowledged in the evaluation, this follow up was based on the views of the champions, their colleagues and team leaders, and as Greenhalgh et al (2005) cautioned, we cannot make any confident claims that any positive changes were due to the champions' actions alone. The central limitation of the evaluation was that it did not include any perspectives from the families involved. Nonetheless, the evaluation, despite its limitations, appeared to find that the initiative had been positive for the staff involved.

Implementation of the Champions Initiative across Northern Ireland

Based on the NHSCT's experience of developing the use of champions and the subsequent evaluation, it was agreed that this development should be rolled out to the other four trusts. This would become part of the TFNI regional action plan and overseen by the Regional Think family sub group.

The first stage of the process was to generate interest and ask each trust to nominate two co-ordinators, one from children's services and one from adult mental health services, who would lead on the development of the Champions Initiative within their trust area. The co-ordinators were to identify four champions locally – two from Children's services and two from adult mental health services, making a total of 20 champions regionally.

A follow-up workshop was convened in May 2015 with all of the nominated champions. The objectives of the workshop were to:

→ agree the elements of an effective learning and development plan to equip the champions to be effective in their role

→ present the feedback from the evaluation of the NHSCT pilot and share the learning from this for future practice

→ explore how NHSCT staff can be used to support the development of the Champions Initiative within the other four trust areas

→ create links with the interface groups in each trust to drive the development and hold staff to account regarding progress

→ raise awareness of the need for evaluation.

Current NHSCT champions framework

→ A Project Steering Group that meets bi-monthly with an agreed terms of reference relating to purpose and function. This is a mix of senior AMH and children's staff to ensure authority for decision-making and to shape and influence direction. This steering group takes direction from the Trust Interface group as outlined in Figure 1.

→ Support groups established for the champions to share information and resources, and present case studies. These are held three or four times per year.

→ Practice days for all champions held three times per year with a focus upon training, guest speakers and sharing learning

→ Specific champion-training to induct them into their role e.g. awareness training for children's staff and AMH on their respective roles and responsibilities, training on perinatal mental health, infant mental health, safeguarding, locally developed protocols, etc. Opportunities to shadow in their respective areas and the identification of a training profile to inform future training opportunities.

Progress to date

Each trust has developed their plans for rolling out the development of the Champions Initiative, and while covering key elements based on the experience of the NHSCT framework above, there are some differences based on trust locality areas relating to how they are currently structured.

However, there are key areas that the other four trusts have agreed:

→ Their use of champions will be based on the NHSCT framework to support a phased approach to this work within each of the other trusts.

→ NHSCT champions would help raise awareness in other trusts regarding their experience of being a champion, its benefits and challenges.

→ A champion training profile would be completed to inform future training opportunities, with champions also contributing to the delivery of training.

→ Opportunities would occur to shadow each other.

→ Create space for both adult mental health services and children's services to learn together.

→ All would link into their interface groups within each trust to oversee the development of the Champions Initiative.

Since the initial meeting in May 2015, throughout the four trust areas there are 91 champions, both adult mental health and children's staff, with the majority from nursing and social work and a smaller proportion from psychiatry, psychology and allied health professionals. With the NHSCT having 67 already, this makes 158 champions within Northern Ireland who are either practising champions, or who are already signed up and undergoing induction to the Champions Initiative. They are meeting regularly through workshops and training events to share the learning together. Some trusts have created specific steering groups based on the NHSCT framework while others have used existing forums in strengthening connectivity with this development.

Conclusion

The work to develop the champions within the other four trusts is moving forward steadily and is one method within a range of initiatives within TFNI that will help to increase knowledge and skills in providing a family-focused approach. The benefits of collaborative working between adult mental health and children's services should prove positive, when there are parental mental health issues within families. The opportunity to share learning, the ability to discuss interface issues and having a better understanding of each other's respective roles and responsibilities within this learning environment can only have benefits.

The development of the Champions Initiative should identify routine and reliable partnership working, recognise each other's contribution within the multi-disciplinary setting, and acknowledge the benefits this brings to the person's recovery and the well-being of their family members.

The evidence for this will arise through the evaluation of the Champions Initiative within adult mental health and children's services. This will be part of the three-year workplan under TFNI. This workplan will see a series of audits, service evaluations and research being identified against specific TFNI work areas to show the value of using the Family Model in practice, and evidence of the impact of the different methods applied as outlined in the three-year workplan.

References

Braithwaite J, Marks D & Taylor N (2014) Harnessing implementation science to improve care quality and patient safety: a systematic review of targeted literature. *International Journal for Quality in Health Care* **26** (3) 321–329.

Cabassa LJ (2016) Implementation Science: Why It Matters for the Future of Social Work. *Journal of Social Work Education* **52** sup 1, S38–S50.

Campbell J, Davidson G & Donnelly M (2013) The Integrated Service in Northern Ireland, in T O'Connor (Ed.) *Integrated Care for Ireland in an International Context*. Cork: Oak Tree Press.

Davidson G, Duffy J, Barry L, Curry P, Darragh E & Lees J (2012) Championing the interface between mental health and child protection: evaluation of a service initiative to improve joint working in Northern Ireland. *Child Abuse Review* **21** (3) 157–172.

Donaghy M (2016) Think family, Northern Ireland. In: Diggins M (Ed) *Parental Mental Health and Child Welfare Work, Vol 1*. Brighton and Hove: Pavilion Publishing & Media.

Falkov A (2012) *The Family Model Handbook*. Brighton and Hove: Pavilion Publishing & Media.

Greenhalgh T, Robert G, Bate P, Macfarlane F & Kyriakidou O (2005) *Diffusion of innovations in health service organisations: a systematic literature review*. Oxford: Blackwell Publishing.

Hendy J & Barlow J (2012) The role of the organisational champion in achieving health system change. *Social Science and Medicine* **74** (3) pp348–355.

Independent Inquiry Panel to the Western & Eastern Health and Social Services Boards (2008) *Report of the Independent Inquiry Panel to the Western and Eastern Health and Social Services Boards*. Belfast: EHSSB.

Iles V & Sutherland K (2001) *Organisational Change: A review for health care managers, professionals and researchers*. London: National Coordinating Centre for the Service Delivery and Organisation.

National Institute of Clinical Excellence (2007) *How to Change Practice: Understand, identify and overcome barriers to change*. London: NICE.

Schon D (1963) Champions for radical new inventions. *Harvard Business Review* **42** 77–86.

Shaw EK, Howard J, West DR, Crabtree BF, Nease DE, Tutt B & Nutting PA (2012) The role of the champion in primary care change efforts: from the State Networks of Colorado Ambulatory Practices and Partners (SNOCAP). *Journal of the American Board of Family Medicine* **25** (5) 676–685.

Social Care Institute of Excellence (2009) *Think Child, Think Parent, Think Family: A guide to parental mental health and child welfare*. London: SCIE.

Social Services Inspectorate (2006) *Child Protection Overview Report 'Our Children and Young People – Our Shared Responsibility: Inspection of Child Protection Services in Northern Ireland'*. Belfast: Department of Health, Social Services and Public Safety.

Warrick DD (2009) Developing organization change champions: a high payoff investment! *Organizational Development Practitioner* **41** (1) 14–19.

Working in Two Worlds

Chris McCree

This article will describe the positive contribution that the creation of an adult mental health safeguarding children's manager has made to implementing and sustaining a 'Think Family' approach in the London Borough of Southwark.

Why did Southwark need someone to fill this role? Developing and sustaining a multi-agency strategy to drive through change at a local level was highlighted as good practice in 'Think Child, Think Parent, Think Family: A guide to parental mental health and child welfare' (SCIE, 2009). Central to Southwark's 'Think Family' strategy has been the joint funding of a dedicated adult mental health safeguarding children's manager.

If you are reading this journal, the chances are that you are already committed to 'Think Family' values, and so expounding on the benefits of such an approach is perhaps redundant. Instead, the issue becomes one of how to get such a model off the ground and how do you sustain it?

I am writing this article as I believe my experience may be of value in answering those questions. I am the first person to be appointed to the role of adult mental health safeguarding children's manager in Southwark and have now been in post for eight years. I am jointly managed by the mental health trust and the Children Social Care (CSC) service. My professional background is in nursing and I have worked in community services both managing a community mental health team (CMHT) and working as a practitioner with staff and families involved with mental health services for many years.

In this article I plan to set out the context in which the post was developed, the intended aims and objectives of the role and how it fits into the wider 'Think Family' strategy in Southwark. I will then describe what has been implemented and include some quotes from other professionals about what they think the role has achieved. I will conclude with what I have learned from taking on the role, including what attributes I think have been essential to doing the job well.

The context in which the role was developed

The statistics below helped those of us committed to a 'think family' approach demonstrate the need for both a strategic approach and the establishment of a dedicated post.

Nationally, we were aware there were approximately 1.7 million people in the UK's adult population suffering from mental health problems, with 2.5 million children living in these families. The evidence suggests, in fact, that mental health problems are most prevalent among adults when they have children. We also know that levels of depression are high in lone parent families and among young parents (Parker et al, 2008).

Around one third of the children known to CAMHs have a parent with an adult mental health problem (Department of Health, 2012). Anecdotally we understand that, despite significant under-reporting, approximately 25% of referrals to children's social care concern children of parents with mental health difficulties. This proportion of referrals was higher when there were concerns about child protection. Furthermore, information from the last Children in Need census showed that, where domestic violence was a problem, parental mental health was twice as likely to feature.

Domestic violence, which includes violence aimed at children or other adults in the household, was the most common factor identified at end of assessment for children in need –49.6% of children in need as of 31st March 2016 had domestic violence as a factor identified at end of assessment, followed by mental health at 36.6%, which incorporates mental health of the child or other adults in the family/household (Department of Education, 2016).

There currently exists a growing body of literature that charts the worrying divide between adult mental health services and children's services. There have been particular problems in the working relationships between adult mental health workers and children and families social workers.

When we began to consider developing the role of adult mental health safeguarding children's manager, the picture in Southwark was not dissimilar to the national situation outlined above. For us, the concerns were heightened by two tragic child deaths, consideration of which pointed to evidence of:

→ poor communication between adult's and children's services about the nature of concerns, risks and appropriate responses

→ mutual negative stereotypes held by children and families workers about parents with mental health problems and those held by mental health workers about the role of children's social care, all of which contributed to a lack of understanding of roles and responsibilities

→ failure by some adult mental health workers to understand their responsibility to identify and manage child protection issues in the families they were working with

→ a lack of understanding of the professional and legal context in which workers from both services were operating

→ structural differences in the organisation of the two services that inhibited communication

→ The absence of a shared understanding of the impact of mental health on families leading to different emphases in assessment and service provision, particularly in the area of risk management.

What were the solutions?

Southwark's decision to develop a multi-agency 'Think Family' strategy was reinforced by our involvement in the work being undertaken by the Social Care Institute for Excellence (SCIE) to develop the national guidance Think Child, Think Parent, Think Family: A guide to parental mental health and child welfare work (SCIE, 2009).

The experience of working alongside other authorities addressing similar issues but from differing standpoints and with differing priorities was enormously energising. Southwark's involvement as a participation site in the development of the SCIE guidance, and subsequently as an implementation pilot site, provided a welcome impetus for our efforts by holding the involved authorities to account and encouraging the exchange of ideas.

The SCIE implementation site evaluation also highlighted that commitment by senior representatives from the key agencies, in this case children's social care and adult mental health, were crucial in achieving an effective strategic response in order to develop a shared understanding of the issues and interventions required. Insights such as this fuelled our decision to form a strategic group that included representatives from children's social care, adult mental health services, a primary care trust and child and adolescent mental health services (CAMHS) alongside the voluntary sector. Crucially, parents who were users of mental health services and young carers contributed fully in this process, thanks to the efforts and encouragement of Southwark Mind and Action for Children. The local safeguarding children board were also fully supportive of the initiative.

This strategic group undertook a review of recent literature, particularly relating to best-practice approaches, and we drew on the resources developed by SCIE including the Parental Mental Health Network, and visited other local authorities that had successfully addressed similar problems.

Adult mental health safeguarding children's manager post

Central to the strategy was the creation of an adult mental health safeguarding children's manager post. In Southwark's case, this position was to be a dedicated post jointly funded by the mental health trust and the local authority. This was critical because it enabled access to both organisations. Reflection among peers in other local authorities who have initiated similar positions confirms that where the post sits is much less important than strong formal commitment to joint funding.

The aim of the post was to help implement a range of changes stemming in part from the findings of recent serious case reviews, and further developed by the strategic group, based on their knowledge of local need and experience.

In summary, the aim was to improve services to the children of Southwark affected by parental mental ill health by:

→ implementing the Southwark Family Strategy[1] and the Joint Service Protocol to meet the needs of children whose parents experience mental health problems

→ improving the joint risk assessment for children where parental mental health is a concern

→ developing a family service that addresses the needs for children and parents in a non-stigmatising way

→ improve the understanding of the respective roles of adult mental health teams and children's teams

---

1 http://www.southwark.gov.uk/download/downloads/id/8315/family_strategy (accessed July 2017)

→ identifying and establishing sustainable systems to support the partnership between adult's and children's services e.g. social services, CAMHS, children's centres, adult mental health services and the voluntary sector.

How has this been achieved?

Learning and development

As part of my responsibilities I commissioned, and on occasion delivered, a locally relevant training schedule over several years, which is on-going. This has enabled me to address and embed the principles of a 'Think Family' approach across services as well as to influence the attitudes of staff and their understanding. I have used a variety of training methods and approaches, reflecting the range of experience and expertise within the different services. I was consequently involved in delivering some aspects of training and commissioning others, in particular the *Crossing Bridges* training (Mayes *et al*, 1998).

We recognised it was important to provide both single agency and multi-agency training so that staff had the opportunity to reflect in a safe space on the parameters of their role and to fully understand the way in which they complimented others' roles. In order to provide specialist training for the adult mental health staff we worked with the Centre for Parent and Child Support to adapt their family partnership training, which provided an opportunity for staff to understand the issues and to increase their skills and confidence in working with families. Encouraging staff to remaining curious about every member of the family's life is, in my opinion, key to improving the family's experience.

'I found this really helpful to build relationships with colleagues in social care and strengthen understanding of our professional roles to overcome barriers in working together.'
Team manager

'Family Partnership Model' training introduced to me the concept of 'constructs' and taught me skills as a practitioner to support shifting parents constructs in order to achieve change for families. I have found these skills have been beneficial in maintaining engagement with parents who have a history of disengaging from services. It's developed my confidence in approaching hard-to-reach families.'
Adult mental health practitioner

Service developments

I established and I manage the parental mental health service, which played an essential part in furthering the strategy. This service consists of nurses and occupational therapists who have skills and knowledge about adult mental health, child development and family approaches. The team sees families in their own homes and provides either one-to-one or group work. The group work is provided within the children's centres because it was seen as important to improve access to local universal services for hard to reach, vulnerable families. The feedback from children's centres has been extremely positive. As a workforce they have a very strong understanding of child development which underpins their child-focused approach and supports their continued 'Think Family' principles. One effective, and unusual, strategy they have employed to achieve their positive reputation is to undertake the 'lead professional' role in the 'team around the family' process, where appropriate. They have also become very skilled at report writing and have earned the high regard of their child protection colleagues.

'One of the greatest strengths of the Family Strategy and the Parental Mental Health team is it promotes working with users in a non-judgmental and compassionate way.'

Parent feedback

Southwark Safeguarding Children Board

My membership of Southwark Safeguarding Children Board and several subgroups has provided me with opportunities to improve communication between services. This has been achieved by steadfastly maintaining the profile of mental health 'Think Family' approaches, sharing learning and identifying the constraints to joined-up thinking, so as to address them. One way in which we addressed best practice issues was to produce multi-agency protocols on parental mental health, parental substance misuse and parental disability and by continuing to influence relevant guidance and shape practice in line with 'Think Family' approaches. Being a dedicated post holder working across adult and children's services, I see the role as making the intellectual connections between what might appear disparate initiatives – challenging 'silo thinking' and ensuring a family perspective is considered.

'These initiatives have influenced and continue to influence the direction of Trust thinking and planning.'
Senior manager Local Safeguarding Children Board

Audits and assurance

Undertaking single and multi-agency audits has helped me to reinforce with staff the centrality to the workload of both services of parental mental health and child welfare issues. It has also provided me with the data to identify the continuing need to address these issues in a 'Think Family' way. At a time of economic stringency we are all being asked to 'do more with less'. While significant improvements have been made it is evident to me that high staff turnover and increasing demands on time and resources means it is still as important as ever to keep this concern high on the agenda.

Supervision and support

A fundamental aspect of my role is to provide advice, consultation and both individual and group supervision to colleagues across the borough. While the focus of this activity ranges from addressing difficulties in communication between services to finding a shared understanding of risk and available resources, key to all of these conversations is the need to ensure that the children remain central. In my experience, it is the opportunity to quickly access specialist consultation on day-to-day work that helps create and maintain worker confidence in 'Think Family' approaches. Staff consistently feed back to me that they value the opportunity to discuss issues in their daily practice with someone who has experience and expertise in the area of family mental health.

'Having access to Chris really increased my confidence as an AMH worker to talk to a 13-year-old about their experience of their mother's mental health condition.'
Community mental health practitioner

Knowledge base

Maintaining an up-to-date knowledge of resources, thresholds and best practice across CSC and adult mental health services has been crucial to informing assessments of risk and devising appropriate responses. By maintaining expertise in these areas I am able to challenge thinking and correct and address misconceptions. It also enables me to solve problems creatively where appropriate and escalate concerns where it is not.

Multi-agency safeguarding hub

The more recent development of a multi-agency safeguarding hub (MASH) in Southwark has created a further significant role for me. As a regular contributor to the MASH service, I have been afforded the opportunity to critically challenge and advance the robust and consistent sharing of pertinent information. Being personally available to staff and helping them to develop their reflective skills has helped to maintain the profile of my role. It has also meant that I have been able to contribute to improved decision-making for families experiencing parental mental ill health, be that sign-posting to early help services, escalation to CSC or referral to adult mental health services.

One MASH professional had this to say:

'As a multi agency safeguarding hub the people we work with and serve as clients are equally diverse as the other. What is fundamental within the MASH however is the passion of those working in here and nowhere is that clearer than in the work and dedication shown by this post holder. Her impact, influence and sharing of her passion for the work she carries out to get results that help those most in need is evident on a daily basis. Mental health plays an integral part in the on-going work being undertaken within the MASH and long may this continue. In some respects the post provides a very tangible interface between diverse workforces and is seen to enhance the core business of the key agencies. It is evident ... that a key component of this post is to not only help practitioners manage their statutory responsibilities but also to improve practice responses. It is in part a measure of the success of this post that it has, over time, become embedded and is seen as a vital contribution to improving the lives of some of the most vulnerable Southwark residents.'

Service user involvement

One area of development of which I am particularly proud is the parent and young people's involvement in all aspects of implementation. We were particularly fortunate in having access to the views of parents who were service users through the local MIND group. We funded a facilitator from Southwark MIND to gather the views of other service users in a number of ways. The importance of their contribution was captured on film, through a grant from the Maudsley Charitable trust, which has been used widely in training. This enabled us to ensure that staff truly understood the complex range of feelings and experiences of services users.

No one says congratulations

The film helped parents to explain what had happened to them in Southwark services and what they wanted to happen to themselves and other parents in the future. This enabled staff to understand better what it feels like to be a parent accessing mental health services, and to gain confidence in knowing what it is parents need from services.

'When I began working with Chris in 2007 the overwhelming sense was that staff in the Trust believed people with mental problems didn't have children. This, thanks to Chris' tireless work, is no longer the case.'
Parent and former service user

What have I learnt?

It has become apparent to me that the success of this post is due to a combination of being a component of a wider family strategy along with the on-going commitment from all service areas and senior management. There were, furthermore, the professional and personal attributes and experience that I brought to the post.

My experience as a nurse within the adult mental health setting with a particular interest in the area of parental mental health and providing a think family model, could be readily undertaken by a professional from a different discipline. However, it is apparent to me and those I work alongside that this is a post that requires a range of seemingly opposing qualities – diplomacy and the willingness to challenge, pragmatism and creativity, an ability to ask awkward questions and yet be sensitive to the answers.

As well as the ability to challenge in order to keep parental mental health on the agenda, I also needed to be mindful of the context people are working in, be available and flexible, pay attention to what is going on around me, keep my knowledge up-to-date on a range of issues, understand what is going on elsewhere and recognise when and what you need to learn from others. I have needed to be repetitive, not only because of the on-going staff changes that services experience, but also because staff need the space and opportunity to develop and be reminded of the approaches that might help.

But above everything else, I would suggest you need to be open and not defensive; you need the resilience I would wish for every family.

However, the work is not yet done and a range of initiatives remain in progress. I have saved **Guidance for parents, children and staff** to the end in order to give the last word – to speak to the families experiencing parental mental health. One way we hope to make their experience better is by way of a series of leaflets setting out for parents and staff the importance of talking to children about their parents' mental health issue and having information for children and young people in order to help them understand what is happening.

In conclusion I have to say how amazing it has felt to have been supported in the development of this role, to be allowed to work across complex organisations. To be welcomed and supported to do the work has been a fantastic opportunity and one that I believe has made a difference to its implementation and value.

References

Department for Education (2016) *Characteristics of Children in Need: 2015 to 2016* [online]. Available at: https://www.gov.uk/government/uploads/system/uploads/attachment_data/file/564620/SFR52-2016_Main_Text.pdf (accessed July 2017).

Department of Health (2012) *Our Children Deserve Better: Prevention pays* [online]. Chief Medical Officer's annual report 2012. Available at: https://www.gov.uk/government/publications/chief-medical-officers-annual-report-2012-our-children-deserve-better-prevention-pays (accessed July 2017).

Mayes K, Diggins M & Falkov A (1998) *Crossing Bridges: Training resources for working with mentally ill parents and their children.* Brighton: Pavilion Publishing and Department of Health.

Parker G, Beresford B, Clarke S, Gridley K, Pitman R, Spiers G & Light K (2008) *Technical report for SCIE Research Review on the prevalence and incidence of parental mental health problems and the detection, screening and reporting of parental mental health problems* [online]. Available at: https://www.york.ac.uk/inst/spru/research/pdf/SCIEReview1.pdf (accessed June 2017).

SCIE (2009) *Think Child, Think Parent, Think Family: A guide to parental mental health and child welfare work.* London: Social Care Institute for Excellence.

Research digest

Research digest

Paul DS Ross (MCLIP)

Introduction

The articles contained within this digest cover recently published research studies from 2015 to 2016 on parental mental health and child welfare. Each study listed in this research digest will include an abstract including information on how to search for current evidence on parental mental health and child welfare using a database or search engine.

The research contained within the digest has been selected to highlight both the topics discussed in this annual and examples of research not included but still relevant to the overall topic. Due to a diverse range of research on parental mental health and child welfare, it has been impossible to include everything. Instead, this digest offers a snapshot of current research and the reader is recommended to conduct their own searches at time of reading.

This research digest has been compiled using Social Care Online, 'the UK's largest database of information and research on all aspects of social care and social work' (SCIE), and through subject expert recommendations. This was complemented by additional searches on Medline.

To find up-to-date research on parental mental health and child welfare, visit social care online (http://www.scie-socialcareonline.org.uk/) using the following search terms: *parental mental health* AND *children*, in either the basic or advance search facility, or you could visit Google Scholar or ProQuest Databases, EBSCO or Ovid, or publisher journal sites such as Pavilion, Wiley, Ingentaconnect, Taylor Francis or Emerald etc.

Research abstracts

A framework for the prevention and mitigation of injury from family violence in children of parents with mental illness and substance use problems

Hartney E & Barnard DK (2015) A framework for the prevention and mitigation of injury from family violence in children of parents with mental illness and substance use problems. *Aggression and Violent Behavior* (25) Part B. 354- 362.

Recognising the need for a more comprehensive approach to preventing child homicides that result from family violence, the authors applied Haddon's three methods of injury prevention to the context of family violence: modification of the agent of injury; identification of control strategies to intervene in the process of injury; and application of the comprehensive Haddon matrix to explore pre-event, event, and post-event strategies addressing the child, parent, and the environment. Examples of evidence-based strategies were identified to support this approach, and innovative strategies were suggested which build on existing approaches applied to other contexts. Recommendations and implications for research and practice are discussed.

Addressing parental mental health within interventions for children: a review

Acri, MC & Hoagwood KE (2015) Addressing parental mental health within interventions for children: a review. *Research on Social Work Practice* **25** (5) 578-586.

Purpose: Untreated parent mental health problems have deleterious effects upon the family, yet caregivers are unlikely to receive services for their emotional health. This review examined treatments and services for children and adolescents that also offered services to parents.

Methods: Child treatment and service studies were included in the present study if they analysed parent symptoms or diagnoses over time, and the intervention contained a parent component. Results: Of 200 studies reviewed, 20 contained a component for the parent and assessed the parent's emotional health at multiple time points. Depression and anxiety were the most commonly studied parental mental health problem; most parent components consisted of behavioural strategies in service of the child's psychological health.

Conclusion: Major shifts in health care policy affecting mental health services provide an opportunity to create integrated and coordinated health and behavioural health systems. Attention must be given to ensure that the workforce of providers, the administrative structures, and the reimbursement strategies are strengthened and connected to serve the needs of parents/ caregivers and children in order to enhance family outcomes.

Applying the recovery approach to the interface between mental health and child protection services

Duffy J, Davidson G & Kavanagh D (2016) Applying the recovery approach to the interface between mental health and child protection services. *Child Care in Practice* **22** (1) 35-49.

There is a range of theoretical approaches which may inform the interface between child protection and adult mental health services. These theoretical perspectives tend to be focused on either child protection or mental health with no agreed integrating framework. The interface continues to be identified, in research, case management reviews and inquiry reports, as complex and problematic. This article proposes that more positive, integrated approaches to service user engagement, risk assessment and management may lead to better outcomes in working with families experiencing parental mental health problems and child protection concerns. It is proposed that the recovery approach, increasingly used in mental health services, can inform the processes of engagement, assessment and intervention at the mental health and child protection interface. The article provides a critical overview of the recovery approach and compares it with approaches typifying interventions in child protection work to date. Relevant research and inquiries are also examined as a context for how to more effectively respond to cases where there are issues around parental mental health problems and child protection. The article concludes with case material to illustrate the potential application of the recovery approach to the interface between mental health and child protection services.

Clinical Effectiveness of Family Therapeutic Interventions Embedded in General Pediatric Primary Care Settings for Parental Mental Health: A systematic review and meta-analysis

Cluxton-Keller F, Riley A, Noazin S, Umoren M, Riley AW & Umoren MV (2015) Clinical Effectiveness of Family Therapeutic Interventions Embedded in General Pediatric Primary Care Settings for Parental Mental Health: A Systematic Review and Meta-analysis. *Clinical Child & Family Psychology Review* **18** (4) 395-412.

The aim of this systematic review and meta-analysis was to synthesise the available evidence on embedded family therapy interventions in paediatrics and impacts on parental mental health and family functioning outcomes. The Cochrane Collaboration guidelines for systematic reviews and meta-analysis were used for this study. Six electronic databases were searched for randomized controlled trials and cluster randomized trials. The Cochrane Collaboration's Risk of Bias Tool and GRADE system were used to rate the quality of evidence of the included studies. The primary outcomes included parental distress, parental depressive symptoms, and dysfunctional parent-child interaction. Fixed effects models showed statistically significant reductions in parental distress at 6-month and 12-month post-intervention in favour of the intervention group. Family therapy model, intervention level, delivery modality, and dosage moderated intervention impacts on parental distress. Fixed effects models showed statistically significant reductions in parental depressive symptoms and in dysfunctional parent-child interaction in favour of the intervention group. Family therapy interventions can be successfully embedded in general paediatric primary care, and intended outcomes are achieved in this setting. Recommendations for future research and implications for policy development are discussed.

Factors that may Facilitate or Hinder a Family-Focus in the Treatment of Parents with a Mental Illness

Lauritzen C, Reedtz C, Doesum K & Martinussen M (2015) Factors that may Facilitate or Hinder a Family-Focus in the Treatment of Parents with a Mental Illness. *Journal of Child & Family Studies* **24** (4) 864-871.

Children with mentally ill parents are at risk of developing mental health problems themselves. To enhance early support for these children may prevent mental health problems from being transmitted from one generation to the next. The sample (N = 219) included health professionals in a large university hospital, who responded to a web-based survey on the routines of the mental health services, attitudes within the workforce capacity, worker's knowledge on the impact of parental mental illness on children, knowledge on legislation concerning children of patients, experience, expectations for possible outcomes of change in current clinical practice and demographic variables. A total of 56 % reported that they did not identify whether or not patients had children. There were no significant differences between the groups (identifiers and non-identifiers) except for the two scales measuring aspects

of knowledge, i.e., Knowledge Children and Knowledge Legislation where workers who identified children had higher scores. The results also showed that younger workers with a medium level of education scored higher on Positive Attitudes. Furthermore, workers who reported to have more knowledge about children and the impact of mental illness on the parenting role were less concerned about a child-focussed approach interfering with the patient-therapist relation.

Family resilience in families where a parent has a mental Illness

Power J, Goodyear M, Maybery D, Reupert A, O'Hanlon B, Cuff R & Parlesz A (2016) Family resilience in families where a parent has a mental Illness. *Journal of Social Work* **16** (1) 66-82.

Summary: This study explores the concept of family resilience where a parent has a mental illness. Eleven Australian adults who have grown up in a household with a parent who had a diagnosed mental illness participated in an in-depth interview. The interviews focused on the ways in which these families responded to challenges in everyday life, particularly related to parental mental illness.

Findings: Families developed resilience through processes such as shared humour or regular family rituals and routines. In some cases, open communication about mental illness enabled families to better cope when parents were unwell and to build a greater sense of family connectedness. However, data suggest that parental mental illness potentially creates stress and confusion for families and there are multiple social and cultural barriers that make it difficult for families to acknowledge and speak openly about mental illness. For participants, resilience tended to be about maintaining a balance between stress/distress and optimism and strength within their family.

Applications: The article highlights the importance of family context when describing resilience, and identifies specific clinical implications for working with families affected by parental mental illness.

Gaining knowledge about parental mental illness: how does it empower children?

Grove C, Reupert A & Maybery Darryl (2015) Gaining knowledge about parental mental illness: how does it empower children? *Child and Family Social Work* **20** (4) 377–386.

This study examined the utility of a digital video disc (DVD) intervention, designed to educate children, whose parents have depression and/or anxiety. Twenty-nine children completed pre- and post-DVD exposure questionnaires, on mental health knowledge and help seeking, and 18 were interviewed about their experiences and use of the DVD. Post-DVD, children's knowledge of mental illness improved. The DVD also challenged mental illness misconceptions. Most children preferred watching the DVD with a parent. The study explains how children utilise information about mental illness.

Goal setting in recovery: families where a parent has a mental illness or a dual diagnosis

Maybery D, Reupert A & Goodyear M (2015) Goal setting in recovery: families where a parent has a mental illness or a dual diagnosis. *Child & Family Social Work* **20** (3) 354–363.

Goal setting is an important element within mental health recovery models; however, parenting and children are rarely recognized in such approaches. This study outlines a family recovery planning model where a parent has a mental health or dual substance and mental health problem. The differences between family types (parent with a mental illness or parent with dual diagnosis) and family members (parent and children) are illustrated in terms of goals across 11 domains. There were a total of 33 parents and 50 children from 10 mental illness and 10 dual diagnosis families. Education and specifically mental health knowledge are important goals across all families and appear especially important for children whose parent has a dual diagnosis. Specific goals and achievement levels for each type of family and parents and children are also outlined. Clear areas for action by clinicians and family members are indicated by this study.

Motherhood and mental distress: personal stories of mothers who have been admitted for mental health treatment

Klausen RK, Karlsson M, Haugsgjerd S & Geir Fagerjord Lorem (2016) Motherhood and mental distress: personal stories of mothers who have been admitted for mental health treatment. *Qualitative Social Work* **15** (1) 103–117.

There is a need for qualitative studies on motherhood and mental distress. Many mothers have a diagnosis of mental illness, and their motherhood exists in constant tension with their distress. This paper focuses on 10 mothers' stories about motherhood in relation to being admitted as mental health service users in three different Norwegian community mental health centres. The study has a narrative approach, and through a thematic analysis of personal stories, the authors emphasise how the 10 women make sense of their experiences of admittance to mental health services in relation to dominant Discourses of good motherhood. Themes identified were: (1) being able to put oneself in the child's shoes; (2) the emotional impact of being admitted; (3) being open with the children about the admission; and (4) being an emotionally available and present mother. Based on the results of our analysis, the authors suggest the mothers experienced their distress as a natural reaction to life strains over time, and that they relate to the admissions as interruptions. This underlines the necessity of a more holistic approach, with a support system that focuses on both personal and social aspects of motherhood and mental distress.

Peer connections as an intervention with children of families where a parent has a mental illness moving towards an understanding of the processes of change

Grove C, Reupert A & Maybery D (2015) Peer connections as an intervention with children of families where a parent has a mental illness moving towards an understanding of the processes of change. *Children and Youth Services Review* (48) 177–185.

Prevention and early intervention programmes have been found to impede the transmission of mental illness from parents to children. However, the extant processes of change in such programmes are less clear. This study focuses on the impact of a peer support programme developed for children and adolescents who have a parent with a mental illness and examines the processes of change which might promote

positive outcomes for youth. A mixed methods research approach was employed with participants aged between 8 and 12 years old; 69 completed pre- and post-questionnaires and 18 of these same participants engaged in telephone interviews post programme. Results demonstrate improved mental health knowledge and children reported that they were more likely to use an anonymous telephone helpline after attending the programme. Children indicated that the programme provided a place of respite from caring for their parent with a mental illness, an opportunity to connect with peers, and a positive change in perception of their parent's mental illness. The reported findings are moving towards an understanding of the process of change in programmes.

Randomized controlled trial of parent-infant psychotherapy for parents with mental health problems and young infants

Fonagy P, Sleed M & Baradon T (2016) Randomized controlled trial of parent-infant psychotherapy for parents with mental health problems and young infants. *Infant Mental Health Journal* **2** (37) 97–114.

There is a dearth of good-quality research investigating the outcomes of psychoanalytic parent-infant psychotherapy (PIP). This randomized controlled trial investigated the outcomes of PIP for parents with mental health problems who also were experiencing high levels of social adversity and their young infants (<12 months). Dyads were clinically referred and randomly allocated to PIP or a control condition of standard secondary and specialist primary care treatment (n = 38 in each group). Outcomes were assessed at baseline and at 6-month and 12-month follow-ups. The primary outcome was infant development. Secondary outcomes included parent-infant interaction, maternal psychopathology, maternal representations, maternal reflective functioning, and infant attachment. There were no differential effects over time between the groups on measures of infant development, parent-infant interaction, or maternal reflective functioning. Infant attachment classifications, measured only at the 12-month follow-up, did not differ between the groups. There were favorable outcomes over time for the PIP-treated dyads relative to the control group on several measures of maternal mental health, parenting stress, and parental representations of the baby and their relationship. The findings indicate potential benefits of parent-infant psychotherapy for improving mothers' psychological well-being and their representations of their baby and the parent-infant relationship.

Shared pleasure in early mother-infant interaction: predicting lower levels of emotional and behavioural problems in the child and protecting against the influence of parental psychopathology

Mäntymaa M, Puura K, Luoma I, Latva R, Salmelin RK & Tamminen T (2015) Shared pleasure in early mother-infant interaction: predicting lower levels of emotional and behavioural problems in the child and protecting against the influence of parental psychopathology. *Infant Mental Health Journal* **36** (2) 223–237.

Shared pleasure (SP) was analysed in fifty-eight 2-month-old infants and their mothers in face-to-face interaction (T1, at 2 months). The association of SP with child's emotional and behavioural outcome at 2 years (T2) was examined. SP as a possible protecting factor in the presence of parental psychopathology also was studied. Mean duration of SP moments (SP-MD) was related to subsequent socioemotional outcome of the child: Infants of dyads with longer SP-MD showed fewer internalizing and externalizing problems 2 years later. In hierarchical linear regressions, SP-MD uniquely and significantly contributed to internalizing problems after adjusting for infant and maternal factors and mother's interactive behaviour. SP protected the child against the influence of parental psychopathology. Father's mental health problems during the follow-up increased the child's risk for higher externalizing and internalizing problems, but only among children with short SP-MD at T1. Internalizing symptoms at T2 increased when moving from the category 'no mental health problems' to 'mental health problems in one parent' and further to 'mental health problems in both parents,' but this increase was found only among those with short SP-MD at T1. SP in parent-child interaction is an important feature that fosters positive psychological development and moderates the health effects of other risks such as parental psychopathology.

The effect of social work use on the mental health outcomes of parents and the life satisfaction of children in Britain

Henderson M, Cheung SY, Sharland E & Scourfield J (2015) The effect of social work use on the mental health outcomes of parents and the life satisfaction of children in Britain. *Children and Youth Services Review* (58) 71–81.

This article examines how parental mental health, and in turn children's well-being is related to receiving social work interventions. Using data from the British Household Panel Survey the authors examine factors predicting the likelihood of parental social work use; whether transitions into social work use is associated with an improvement of mental health outcomes of those parents who receive it; and whether parental social work use enhances their children's well-being. Taking advantage of panel data modelling techniques, random and fixed effects models were used to account for the unobserved individual characteristics. The findings indicate that poor health, disability, having more children in household, not being married and more than 35 h of caring responsibilities are all associated with an increase in the likelihood of parental social work use. It also finds that parents who use a social worker report worse mental health outcomes for themselves, and poorer well-being for their children, than those who do not. Possible explanations for these findings are discussed as well as implications for policy makers.

The mother load

Patients Voice (2016) The mother load. *Journal of Paediatrics & Child Health* (523) 347–348.

The author shares her sentiments about the challenges of being a mother of two children with health challenges. She describes her qualities as a competent mother and points out her need of parental mental health care in the same way as pediatricians focus on improving health outcomes for her children. She expresses dismay with being tired of suffering from appointment fatigue and she emphasizes the need for a system that makes it easy for parents to receive mental health support services.

Using the Assessment Framework to measure parental mood: an investigation of the reliability of the Adult Well-Being Scale

Pepping CA, Dawe S & Harnett PH (2016) Using the Assessment Framework to measure parental mood: an investigation of the reliability of the Adult Well-Being Scale. *Child and Family Social Work* (2) 1144–54.

The adoption of evidence-based practice in social work has been widely promoted in recent years and with this, a growing emphasis on the evaluation of practice using well-validated and reliable measurement processes. The Department of Health's 'Framework for the Assessment of Children in Need and their Families' in the UK includes quantitative measures that form part of a systematic assessment of the needs of children and their families that includes assessment of parenting capacity and parental emotional state. The measure selected to assess parental mood was originally known as the Irritability, Depression and Anxiety Scale, and has been renamed within the Assessment Framework as the Adult Well-Being Scale. This instrument is designed to assess depression, anxiety, and inward and outward irritability. However, there has been relatively little contemporary evaluation of the reliability and validity of the measure, and the extent to which it measures the four constructs it is designed to assess. This research therefore conducted extensive analyses of the reliability, validity and underlying factor structure of the Adult Well-Being Scale. The four subscales did not demonstrate sound psychometric properties. At best a total score may be used as an indicator of 'overall psychological distress'.

Power J, Cuff R, Jewell H, McIlwaine, O'Neil I & U'Ren G (2015) Working in a family therapy setting with families where a parent has a mental illness: practice dilemmas and strategies. *Journal of Family Therapy* (37) 4 546–562.

There is strong evidence supporting the benefits of family work, for both parents and children, in the treatment of parental mental illness. However, there has been only limited research on the implementation of family work in settings outside the mental health sector, such as family therapy or family counselling services, where mental illness may not be the primary presenting issue for a family. This article reports on a qualitative study that explored the experiences of family therapists working with families affected by parental mental illness. The article focuses on dilemmas clinicians faced integrating discussions about parental mental illness into family sessions. The findings support the need for clinicians to have appropriate training in family work related to mental health issues and also to develop the skill set needed to actively introduce, negotiate and explore the topic of mental illness with families.

Resources

Ross PDS (2015) Locating evidence for practice. In: Webber M. Applying research evidence in social work practice. London: Palgrave (pp22-43). London: Palgrave

Useful tools and resources

Useful tools and resources

Information and resources for parents, children and families, carers and professionals

The Social Care Institute for Excellence (SCIE) Parental mental health and child welfare resources

SCIE's comprehensive suite of resources includes: a review of the evidence about parental mental health and child welfare work, cross-cutting health and social care accredited guidance, e-learning, and implementation learning. SCIE (2015): https://www.scie.org.uk/children/parentalmentalhealthandchildwelfare/

Keeping the Family in Mind Resource Pack (2nd Edition) (Wardale L, 2007)

http://www.barnardos.org.uk/keeping_family_in_mind_flyer.pdf

COPMI – Children of Parents with a Mental Illness: mental health information and resources for Australian parents, children, families, carers and health professionals

http://www.copmi.net.au

Kidstime Foundation

The foundation brings together young people, nurses and psychiatrists, to develop programmes aimed at promoting resilience in the children who are affected by parental mental illness and to help reduce the stigma associated with mental ill-health in general. Projects currently available at Kidstime include: 'When a Parent has a Mental Illness' film, Being Seen And Heard, The Who Cares Project, Kidstime Workshops and Working together. http://kidstimefoundation.org

The Children's Society – Engage toolkit – whole family working

The Engage toolkit brings together a range of resources to improve health and social care practice in working with and responding to the needs of the whole family. www.engagetoolkit.org.uk/health-social-care/resources-support-whole-family-working

The Children's Society – Include programme – Supporting young carers and their families

Information and resources for all professionals.
http://www.youngcarer.com/?file=2010102142315.htm

Mind – for better mental health

http://www.mind.org.uk

Mind – Parenting with a mental health problem

Explains difficulties you may face as a parent with a mental health problem, what support is available and suggestions on how to help yourself and your children. Includes information for:

▶ Friends and family

▶ Parenting and mental health

▶ Helping yourself

▶ Helping your children

▶ Support

▶ Crises

▶ Children and care

www.mind.org.uk/information-support/tips-for-everyday-living/parenting-with-a-mental-health-problem/#.WQC9VRSQKX0

YoungMinds – The voice for young people's mental health and wellbeing

http://www.youngminds.org.uk

Mental Health Foundation – Dedicated to finding and addressing the sources of mental health problems

www.mentalhealth.org.uk

Young Carers Research Group – Loughborough University

Downloadable publications, resources, current research, Young Carers' needs analysis, publications, Young Carers' Mental Health.
http://www.lboro.ac.uk/microsites/socialsciences/ycrg/

Carers UK – making life better for carers

http://www.carersuk.org/help-and-advice

Carers Trust – action – help – advice

www.carers.org.uk

Carers Trust – Whole family approach – practice examples

This is collection of practice examples to support those who commission or develop services think about how to deliver creative and effective services locally. https://professionals.carers.org/whole-family-approach-practice-examples

Free Social Work Tools and Resources: Social Workers Toolbox for Direct Work with Children and Adults by Social Workers

http://www.socialworkerstoolbox.com

Services

Anna Freud Centre – The Early Years Parenting Unit (EYPU)

The Early Years Parenting Unit (EYPU) is a specialist service offering assessment and therapy for parents with personality disorders/difficulties with babies and children under the age of five who are subject to a Child in Need or Child Protection plan, or who are on the edge of care. www.annafreud.org/services-schools/services-for-children-young-people-families/early-years-parenting-unit/

NSPCC – Family SMILES – Supporting children living with parents with mental health issues

Family SMILES aims to help children aged eight to 14 to build self-esteem, resilience and life skills. Family SMILES also works with parents to help them understand the impact of their illness on their child and to improve their parenting skills to provide a safe, secure and supportive family environment. www.nspcc.org.uk/services-and-resources/services-for-children-and-families/family-smiles/

Family Action: Building Bridges

Building Bridges is Family Action's home-based family support service that works with families that might have problems such as parental mental health issues, a young carer at home, difficulties in parenting, children with mental health or behaviour difficulties, relationship issues, safeguarding issues and financial and material hardship. Building Bridges works holistically in the family home with parents and children to develop an action plan that will help families build stronger and more positive futures. https://www.family-action.org.uk/building-bridges/

Assessment, planning and prevention

Interface – Schools; vulnerable children audit tool

Interface have worked with schools to develop an electronic tool to help school leaders, governors, teachers, support-staff and multi-agency partners to identify vulnerable children and their families and work more effectively and efficiently with them.
www.interfaceenterprises.co.uk/consultancy/schools-vulnerable-children-audit-tool/

Identifying and Recognising the Needs of Young Carers – New Mental Health Questionnaire and Screening Tool – The Young Carers Research Group Loughborough.

The Young Carers Research Group has launched a new questionnaire and screening tool to help researchers and health, social care and education professionals estimate the prevalence of young carers in a given area and to identify their needs. The YC-QST-20 (Mental Health) is intended to be used as a research and screening tool among children who may be living with, and/or caring for, a relative in the home (such as a parent, grandparent or sibling) with a mental health problem/mental illness. The YC-QST-20 (Mental Health) is also intended to gauge children's level of understanding about their relative's illness/mental health problem, the nature and extent of children's caring responsibilities and their needs as carers.
www.lboro.ac.uk/microsites/socialsciences/ycrg/resources.html

InterAct

A new model of working with children and young people who care for someone with a mental health problem: Gloucestershire Young Carers Project: InterAct. For more information visit www.glosyoungcarers.org.uk
To download the flyer, visit: www.lboro.ac.uk/microsites/socialsciences/ycrg/youngCarersDownload/InterAct%20Poster_A3.pdf

Message in a Bottle – Barnardos Action with Young Carers Liverpool

The Message in a Bottle Pack (which contains medical information in a pot that has been adapted from the Lions Club original to be child-friendly and personalised) designed in partnership with families, helps them to think and prepare for any medical and family emergencies, relieving many of the concerns that young carers have, including the belief that they are responsible for their parent's ill-health. Together, an advance statement and message in a bottle support plan can help to support the whole family.
For further information visit www.liverpoolcamhs.com/support/barnardos-action-with-young-carers/

For more information on Lions Clubs International, visit www.lionsclubs.co/MemberArea/?p=314message-in-a-bottle

Promoting family contact when a parent is in hospital

Mersey Care NHS Trust and Barnardo's Family Rooms – Family Rooms for young carers visiting relatives using inpatient mental health services

Mersey Care NHS Trust runs this service in partnership with Barnardo's Keeping the Family in Mind (KFIM) – a project to engage young carers in the delivery of services for families affected by mental health issues. This is part of the Barnardo's Action with Young Carers (AWYC) service in Liverpool.

Family rooms provide a safe, comfortable and homely environment for children, young people and their families when they visit a family member staying in a specialist mental health, learning disability or substance misuse service. The family rooms have all been designed with young carers to make sure they are in an environment which is a home away from home. The services has been running since 2001.

For further information:
Ann Hanlon
Business Development Lead, Trust Wide Women and Think Family Lead, Mersey Care NHS Foundation Trust
Email: Ann.Hanlon@ merseycare.nhs.uk

Louise Wardale
Keeping the Family in Mind Coordinator
Barnardos's Action with Young Carers Liverpool
Email: louise.wardale@barnardos.org.uk

For further information and useful links see:
www.merseycare.nhs.uk/our-services/think-family/

Mersey Care NHS Trust – Thinking Family in High Secure Services

Think Family is showcased in a film produced by Secure Services Division for family visiting arrangements at Ashworth Hospital Mersey Care NHS Trust – web reference to view an online film for families and children can be found at: www.merseycare.nhs.uk/our-services/a-z-of-services/ashworth-high-secure-hospital/bringing-children-on-visits-to-ashworth-hospital/

Leaflets and factsheets

Parental Mental Illness: The impact on children and adolescents: Information for parents, carers and anyone who works with young people (2012)

The Royal College of Psychiatrists
www.rcpsych.ac.uk/healthadvice/parentsandyouthinfo/parentscarers/
parentalmentalillness.aspx

Parents and Youth Info Index

An index providing specifically tailored information for young people, parents, teachers and carers about mental health from the The Royal College of Psychiatrists.
www.rcpsych.ac.uk/healthadvice/parentsandyouthinfo.aspx

Mental Health and Growing Up: Factsheets for parents, teachers and young people

The Royal College of Psychiatrists (2012)
www.rcpsych.ac.uk/usefulresources/publications/books/rcpp/9781908020468.aspx

So your Mum or Dad has a mental illness

Two leaflets for children and young people whose parents are experiencing mental illness. Children and Young People's Strategic Partnership (CYPSP) Northern Ireland & Participation Network Supporting the Public Sector to engage with children and young people:
www.cypsp.org/wp-content/uploads/2014/08/Think_Family_Leaflet_Childrens.pdf
www.cypsp.org/wp-content/uploads/2014/08/Think_Family_Leaflet_Young_People_(2).pdf

Training and workforce development

The Family Model: An integrated approach to support mentally ill parents and their children

www.thefamilymodel.com

The Centre for Parent and Child Support and the Family Partnership Model

South London and Maudsley NHS Foundation Trust
www.cpcs.org.uk

Interface Enterprises Ltd

Interface is a national provider of specialist support, training, information and resources for those working to transform the lives of vulnerable children and families. Their aim is to enhance capacity and expertise in local areas and they do this across priority areas of service delivery for communities, children and vulnerable families. www.interfaceenterprises.co.uk/about-us/

Interface Enterprises Ltd – C-Change – Capacity to Change

Interface Enterprises have partnered with the University of Bristol to deliver national training to support the embedding of the C-Change Capacity to Change approach. C-Change is a flexible approach to assessing parents' capacities to change where the children are in need or at risk of maltreatment. www.interfaceenterprises.co.uk/training/skills-training/course/c-change-capacity-to-change

The Meriden Family Programme – NHS

www.meridenfamilyprogramme.com

Anna Freud Centre

Training and Research
www.annafreud.org/training-research/training-and-conferences-overview/

e-Learning: Parental mental health and families (SCIE)

www.scie.org.uk/publications/elearning/parentalmentalhealthandfamilies/index.asp

When a parent has a mental illness

Coping with a parent with a mental illness (film). The Royal College of Psychiatrists www.rcpsych.ac.uk/healthadvice/parentsandyouthinfo/youngpeople/caringforaparent.aspx

Policy and practice guidance

Mental health and behaviour in schools – How to identify and support pupils whose behaviour suggests may have unmet mental health needs

Department for Education

This guidance is for school staff and applies to all schools. It gives advice on:

▶ How and when to refer to the Child and Adolescent Mental Health Services (CAMHS)

- ▶ Supporting children with emotional and behavioural difficulties
- ▶ Strengthening pupil resilience
- ▶ How to identify pupils likely to need extra support
- ▶ Where and how to access community support

www.gov.uk/government/publications/mental-health-and-behaviour-in-schools--2

The Care Act: Transition from childhood to adulthood (SCIE, 2015)

www.scie.org.uk/care-act-2014/transition-from-childhood-to-adulthood/

Transition from children's to adult services – early and comprehensive identification (SCIE, 2015)

www.scie.org.uk/care-act-2014/transition-from-childhood-to-adulthood/early-comprehensive-identification/index.asp

Young carer transition in practice under the Care Act (SCIE, 2015)

www.scie.org.uk/care-act-2014/transition-from-childhood-to-adulthood/young-carer-transition-in-practice/index.asp

Think child, think parent, think family: a guide to parental mental health and child welfare (SCIE, updated 2011)

This guide has not been updated since December 2011. It may not reflect current policy but still provides valuable practice guidance.
www.scie.org.uk/publications/guides/guide30/index.asp

The Family Model Handbook: An integrated approach to supporting mentally ill parents and their children

By Dr Adrian Falkov
This book presents The Family Model approach to working with parental mental illness and effects on family relationships, children's needs and parenting, for clinicians and managers.
Available at: www.pavpub.com/the-family-model-handbook/

COPMI GEMS – The Continuum of Need

Dr Adrian Falkov
The 'Continuum of Need' provides a basis for thinking about levels of need along a theoretical continuum, based on the diversity of individuals' needs within families.
www.copmi.net.au/images/pdf/Research/gems-edition-17-may-2014.pdf

Research

Fatherhood: Briefing 50: Fatherhood: the impact of fathers on children's mental health (2017) Centre for Mental Health

Lorraine Khan
While there is growing awareness about the importance of mothers' mental health, less is known about fatherhood and the impact fathers can have on their children's mental health. *Fatherhood: the impact of fathers on children's mental health*, explores the research available on this topic and highlights the distinct role fathers can play in nurturing good mental health in their children.

Parents with a mental health problem: learning from case reviews

National Society for the Prevention of Cruelty to Children
This briefing highlights risk factors and key learning for improved practice from case reviews where the mental health problems of parents was a key factor. It is based on case reviews published from since 2013. The briefing identifies the following risk factors for practitioners to be aware of: disclosure of suicidal feelings; threats to kill; stress factors; domestic abuse; drug or alcohol misuse; and lack of engagement with services. Pointers to improve practice include: giving better consideration of the impact of mental health issues on parenting capacity; the need for children's services and adult services to work together and think of the whole family; listening to parents; having the confidence to question and challenge; and ensuring assessment is a shared task between children's social workers and adult mental health.

Working with families where there is domestic violence, parent substance misuse and/or parent mental health problems. A rapid research review.

Institute of Public Care, Hampshire County Council & Oxford Brookes University
This review provides a summary of the reported prevalence of parent mental illness, parent substance misuse and domestic violence in different cohorts (i.e. the overall population; families subject to child protection procedures or care proceedings; and serious case reviews). It sets out the context for thinking about changes in social work and whole system practice with these families and outlines the findings from research to date about the impact of and 'what works' in relation to each of these elements in isolation as well as collectively.

Keeping the Family in Mind: A briefing on young carers whose parents have mental health problems

Barnardo's
www.barnardos.org.uk/keeping_the_family_in_mind.pdf

Gateways to Evidence that Matters (GEMS)

Children of Parents with a Mental Illness (OPMI)
The aim of the 'Gateways to Evidence that Matters' (GEMS) is to provide a summary of recent Australian and international research concerning children (aged 0-18 years) of parents with a mental illness, their parents and families. While research in this area is growing, there is a lack of evidence-based practice when working with families affected by parental mental illness.

These GEMS have been prepared as a resource for those working in the field, and aim to provide a synthesis of available research that might guide and direct practitioners, and highlight current research and practice gaps. GEMS promotes the collection, interpretation and integration of valid, recent and relevant research from around the world, based on the views and experiences of those researching, working and living with parental mental illness.

www.copmi.net.au/professionals-organisations/what-works/research-summaries-gems

Related publications

Sawyer E & Burton S (2016) A Practical Guide to Early Intervention and Family Support: Assessing needs and building resilience in families affected by parental mental health problems or substance misuse. London: Jessica Kingsley.

This handbook provides practitioners with early intervention techniques and effective support strategies for ensuring the best outcomes for these vulnerable families. Featuring pointers, models and practice examples, this book considers the concept of resilience and effective family support. Assessing the policy context and possible barriers to support, it looks at assessment of need, safeguarding children, minimising negative impact, and most importantly, keeping families together where possible. Drawing on key research on the risks and impacts, it demonstrates the need for a unified approach from a range of adult and children's services.

www.jkp.com/usa/a-practical-guide-to-early-intervention-and-family-support-33895.html/

Reupert A, Maybery D, Nicholson J, Gopfert M & Seeman M (2015) Parental Psychiatric Disorder – Distressed Parents and their Families – 3rd Edition

Cambridge University Press.
Parental Psychiatric Disorder presents an innovative approach to thinking about and working with families where a parent has a mental illness. With 30 new chapters from internationally renowned authors, this new edition presents the current state of knowledge in this critically important field. Issues around prevalence, stigma and systems theory provide a foundation for the book, which offers new paradigms for understanding mental illness in families. The impact of various parental psychiatric

disorders on children and family relationships are summarised, including coverage of schizophrenia, depression, anxiety, substance abuse disorders, eating disorders, personality disorders and trauma. Multiple innovative interventions are outlined, targeting children, parents and families, as well as strategies that foster workforce and organisational development. Incorporating different theoretical frameworks, the book enhances understanding of the dimensions of psychiatric disorders from a multigenerational perspective, making this an invaluable text for students, researchers and clinicians from many mental health disciplines.

www.cambridge.org/gb/academic/subjects/medicine/mental-health-psychiatry-and-clinical-psychology/parental-psychiatric-disorder-distressed-parents-and-their-families-3rd-edition

Aldridge J (2016) Participatory Research: Working with vulnerable groups in research and practice

Policy Press.

Jo Aldridge's new book, *Participatory Research: Working with Vulnerable Groups in Research and Practice*, published by The Policy Press, includes in-depth case studies and examples of participatory research methods that have been used with young carers and their families, as well as with people with profound learning difficulties and unsupported women victims of domestic violence. The book also includes a new Participatory Research Model that provides researchers, academics and students with clear parameters for working more effectively with vulnerable or marginalised groups. The book includes extensive discussion and examination of what is meant by 'vulnerability' in different health, social care and academic contexts, as well as from the perspectives of people defined as 'vulnerable' themselves. More details about the book, including ordering information, can be found here:
https://policypress.co.uk/participatory-research

Loshak R (2013) Out of the Mainstream: Helping the children of parents with a mental illness

Routledge

Out of Mainstream considers how the diverse groups of agencies, specialist teams and groups in the community can work together, even when many barriers may hinder the effective co-working between individuals and these various groups. It is an invaluable resource for psychologists, psychiatrists, social workers, health visitors, mental health nurses, teachers and voluntary sector agency staff.

www.lovereading.co.uk/book/9780415682695/isbn/Out-of-the-Mainstream-Helping-the-Children-of-Parents-with-a-Mental-Illness-by-Rosemary-Loshak.html

CR164. Parents As Patients: Supporting the needs of patients who are parents and their children (2010)

Royal College of Psychiatrists
Free PDF version available at:
www.rcpsych.ac.uk/usefulresources/publications/collegereports/cr/cr164.aspx

Robinson B & Scott S (2007) Parents in Hospital: How mental health services can best promote family contact when a parent is in hospital: Barnardo's

Full report and summary available at: www.barnardos.org.uk/resources/research_and_publications/parents-in-hospital-how-mental-health-services-can-best-promote-family-contact-when-a-parent-is-in-hospital/publication-view.jsp?pid=PUB-1393